About a Boy

Nick Hornby

Level 4

Retold by Anne Collins

Series Editors: Andy Hopkins and Jocelyn Potter

Pearson Education Limited

Edinburgh Gate, Harlow,
Essex CM20 2JE, England
and Associated Companies throughout the world.

Pack ISBN: 978-1-4058-8450-1
Book ISBN: 978-1-4058-8404-4
CD-ROM ISBN: 978-1-4058-8403-7

First published in Great Britain by Victor Gollancz 1988
First edition published 2003
This edition published 2008

5 7 9 10 8 6

Original copyright © Nick Hornby 1988
Text copyright © Penguin Books Ltd 2003
This edition copyright © Pearson Education Ltd 2008
Illustrations by Iván García
The author has asserted her moral right in accordance with the
Copyright Designs and Patents Act 1988

Set in 11/13pt A. Garamond
Printed in China
SWTC/05

Produced for the Publishers by AC Estudio Editorial S.L.

Published by Pearson Education Ltd in association with Penguin Books Ltd,
both companies being subsidiaries of Pearson Plc

For a complete list of the titles available in the Penguin Active Reading series please write to your local
Pearson Longman office or to: Penguin Readers Marketing Department, Pearson Education,
Edinburgh Gate, Harlow, Essex CM20 2JE, England.

Contents

1.1 What's the book about?

Have you seen the film *About a Boy*?

• YES

Match some of the characters from the film with these pictures. What do you remember about the characters?

• NO

Read about some of the characters in the story. Match them with the correct pictures above.

1 ☐ Will is a very rich young man.
2 ☐ Marcus is a boy with problems.
3 ☐ Fiona is Marcus's mum. She's often very sad.
4 ☐ Christine is a tired young mother, a friend of Will.

1.2 What happens first?

Discuss these questions. What do you think? Make notes below.

1 Look at the words in *italics* at the top of page 1. Then look at the picture on page 3. What is Will thinking?
2 Look at the picture on page 6. What are Marcus and the other pupils thinking?
3 Look at the picture on page 17. What is Marcus thinking?

Notes

CHAPTER 1

A Man and a Boy

Will could see only one reason for having children.
When you were old and poor, then they could look after you.

Will Freeman was thirty-six years old and he had never had a job in his life. Sometimes he thought about working. He looked through the job advertisements in newspapers and wrote occasional letters to employers, but he was never invited to interviews.

He didn't mind. He was OK as he was. He was a **cool guy** with a cool lifestyle. He read quite a lot; he saw films in the afternoons; he went running; he cooked nice meals for himself and his friends. When he got bored, he went to Rome or New York or Barcelona for a few days.

Will didn't need to work for money because in 1938 his father had written a very successful Christmas song. Many famous singers had made recordings of this song, and each time Will's father had received **royalties**. Since his death the royalties had come to Will.

So Will had become rich without having to work at all. He was happy with his life. He lived in a nice flat in London and drove a fast car. He liked women and had lots of girlfriends, but he never got too **involved with** them. He preferred to look at other people's lives from the outside, like watching TV. If a relationship with a woman became complicated, he ended it. He wanted to keep his life simple.

In the evenings Will usually went out with friends. These were guys who worked in music shops or belonged to the same sports clubs as Will, or who were part of the same pub-**quiz** team. They weren't close friends – but they were good enough for a drink or a meal.

The evenings were fine, but Will had a lot of free time during the day because all his friends were at work. So he filled the time with different half-hour activities – reading the paper, having a bath, tidying his flat, going to the shops, watching *Countdown*. *Countdown* was an afternoon TV quiz show and it was his favourite programme. Sometimes he wondered how his friends had time to work. How could a person work and have a bath on the same day?

---

cool /kuːl/ (adj) an informal word for a person or thing that you like and admire
guy /gaɪ/ (n) an informal word for a man
royalties /ˈrɔɪəltiz/ (n pl) payments made to the writer of a book or a piece of music, connected to the sales of that work
be/get involved (with) /bi /ˌget ɪnˈvɒlvd wɪð, wɪθ/ to be/become part of someone's life, or part of an activity or event
quiz /kwɪz/ (n) a competition in which you have to answer questions

Will didn't like children. He wasn't interested in them, and he didn't want any responsibility for them. But his friends, John and Christine, had two. The second was a baby girl, born just the week before, and Will had been invited to see her.

When he arrived at John and Christine's flat, there were children's toys everywhere. Pieces of brightly coloured plastic were spread all over the floor, videos lay out of their cases near the TV, a white cloth over the sofa was covered with dirty brown marks ... How could people live like this?

Christine came in holding the new baby while John was in the kitchen making tea. 'This is Imogen,' she said.

'Oh,' said Will. 'Right.' He paused. What did people usually say about babies? 'She's ...' he began, but stopped again. It was no good. He decided to ask Christine about herself instead. 'How are you, Chris?' he asked.

'Well, you know. I'm rather tired.'

'Why? A lot of parties?'

'No. I've just had a baby.'

'Oh. Right.'

John came into the room, carrying three cups of tea. 'Barney's gone to his grandmother's today,' he said, for no reason that Will could understand.

'How's Barney?' Barney was two, and interesting only to his parents, but Will knew he should ask John something.

'He's fine, thanks,' said John. 'He's still getting used to Imogen, but he's lovely.'

Will had met Barney before and knew that he wasn't lovely, but he decided not to say anything.

'What about you, Will?'

'I'm fine, thanks.'

'Don't you want your own family?'

I can't think of anything worse, thought Will. 'Not yet,' he said.

'We're worried about you,' said Christine.

'I'm OK as I am, thanks,' said Will.

'Maybe,' said Christine, and smiled.

Will was beginning to feel very uncomfortable. Why did they want him to have children? Children would make him very unhappy. If John and Christine wanted children, and to be unhappy, that was fine. (Will was sure that John and Christine were very unhappy, even if they didn't realize it.) But why should they want him to be unhappy too?

Will could see only one reason for having children. When you were old and poor, then they could look after you. But Will had plenty of money, so he didn't need toys on the floor or dirty sofas.

John and Christine used to be OK, he thought. Will and a girlfriend had gone out to nightclubs with them once or twice a week, and they had all had a lot of fun. But since John and Christine had had children, everything had changed. Will didn't want to meet Imogen, or hear how Barney was. He didn't want to hear about Christine's tiredness. He decided not to visit them again.

'We were wondering,' said John, 'whether you'd like to be Imogen's **godfather**?' The two of them looked at Will, smiling and waiting for his reply.

Will laughed nervously. 'Godfather?' he said. 'You mean ... church and things? Birthday presents? If you two are killed in an air crash, I'll have to look after her?'

'Yes.'

'You're joking, aren't you?'

---

godfather /ˈgɒdˌfɑːðə/ (n) a man who promises, usually at a religious ceremony, to be responsible for a child's religious education

'No,' said John. 'We've always thought that, deep down inside, you're a very serious and responsible person.'

'Oh, no,' said Will quickly. 'No, I'm not. I'm really a very shallow kind of person. Thank you very much for asking me, but I can't think of anything worse.'

He didn't stay much longer.

◆

Not far away, in the Holloway area of London, a twelve-year-old boy called Marcus was lying in bed, unable to sleep. He was worrying about his mum and his new school.

Marcus's mum was called Fiona, and she and Marcus had only been in London for a few weeks. They had moved there on the first day of the summer holidays because Fiona had got a new job. Before moving to London, they had lived in Cambridge, where Marcus's father, Clive, still lived. Fiona and Clive had separated four years ago.

Marcus thought London was quite boring. He and Fiona hadn't done much in the holidays. They'd been to see *Home Alone 2*, which wasn't as good as *Home Alone 1*. They'd been to have a look at his new school, which was big and horrible. And they'd had lots of talks about London and the changes in their lives. But really they were sitting around waiting for their London lives to begin.

Marcus had had two kinds of life. The first, which had ended when he was eight, was the normal, boring kind, with school and holidays and homework and weekend visits to grandparents. The second kind was more confused because there were more people and places in it: his mother's boyfriends and his dad's girlfriends; flats and houses; Cambridge and London. It was surprising how many things had changed when Fiona and Clive's relationship ended.

But Marcus didn't mind. Sometimes, he thought, he even preferred the second kind of life to the first. It was more exciting. More happened, and that was a good thing.

But now Marcus was very worried about his mum. She had started crying a lot in London – much more than in Cambridge. He didn't know why she cried. He wondered if it was about boyfriends. Marcus didn't mind if his mum had a boyfriend. She was pretty, he thought, and nice, and funny sometimes. He wanted his mum to meet someone who would make her happy.

He couldn't help his mum with her problems, and she couldn't help him with his other big problem – school. His first day at his new London school had been a disaster.

Marcus knew that he was different from most other **kid**s of his age. He wasn't right for schools. Not big secondary schools like the one in London. His school in Cambridge hadn't been so bad. The children there were younger, and there were lots of **weird** kids there, so Marcus hadn't felt uncomfortable.

It was OK not to be right for some things, he thought. He knew that he wasn't right for parties because he was very shy. That wasn't a problem because he didn't have to go to parties. But he had to go to school.

Marcus couldn't talk to his mum about his problems at school, because she couldn't help. She couldn't move him to another school. Even if she did move him, it wouldn't make any difference. He'd still be himself, and that, it seemed to Marcus, was his real problem. The other kids laughed at him because he was weird. They laughed because he had the wrong trousers, the wrong shoes and the wrong haircut.

Marcus knew that he was weird partly because his mum was weird. She was always telling him that clothes and hair weren't important. She didn't want him

kid /kɪd/ (n) an informal word for a child
weird /wɪəd/ (adj) unusual and strange

to watch 'rubbish' TV or listen to 'rubbish' music or play 'rubbish' computer games. All the other kids spent their time doing these things, but Marcus had to argue with his mother for hours and he usually lost. She could explain why it was better for him to listen to singers from the 1960s like Bob Marley and Joni Mitchell. And why it was more important to read books than to play on the Gameboy that his dad had given him.

He was quite happy at home, listening to Joni Mitchell or reading books, but it didn't do him any good at school. It made him different, and because he was different the other kids made him feel uncomfortable.

It wasn't all his mum's fault. Sometimes Marcus just did weird things. Like the singing. He always sang songs to himself inside his head, but sometimes, when he was nervous, the song just came out of his mouth. It had happened in his English lesson on the first day of his new school. The teacher was reading and all the other students in the room were quiet. Suddenly, for no reason at all, Marcus had started to sing, and all the other kids had laughed at him.

CHAPTER 2

SPAT

*Marcus was shocked. What did she mean, they weren't doing each other any good?
She wasn't doing him any good, but what had he done to her?*

Will first saw Angie in a music shop off the Holloway Road. She had lots of thick **blonde** hair, big blue eyes and a lovely sexy voice. She reminded him of Julie Christie, a beautiful film star. Two days later, he saw her again in a café and started a conversation. By the time they had finished their coffee, he had her phone number.

Will was rather surprised that Angie wanted to go out with him. He had never been out with a woman who looked like Julie Christie before. Women like her

didn't go out with men like Will. They went out with other film stars, or lords, or racing drivers.

He learnt the reason over dinner on their first evening out, when Angie told him that she was a single mother with two small kids. It wasn't easy for her to get out and meet new men, and a lot of men didn't like other people's children.

Will wanted to push the table over and run out of the restaurant, but Angie was a very beautiful woman.

'Really, it's no problem. I've never been out with a mum before, and I've always wanted to. I think I'd be good at it.'

'Good at what?'

Right. Good at what? What was he good at? That was the big question which he had never been able to answer. Maybe he would be good at children, although he hated them. Maybe he should give John and Christine and baby Imogen another chance. Maybe he was going to become Uncle Will!

'I don't know. Doing things that kids like.'

For the next few weeks, he was Will the Good Guy, and he loved it. It wasn't even very difficult. He played with Angie's children, and took them to McDonald's and to parks and for a boat trip on the river. It was a very good arrangement, he thought. He had never wanted to be a father, but this was different. He could walk hand-in-hand with a beautiful woman while the

blond(e) /blɒnd/ (adj) pale yellow

7

children played in front of them. Everybody could see him doing it. And at the end of the afternoon, he could go home again if he wanted to.

Angie made Will feel very good about himself. Suddenly he became better-looking, a better lover, a better person. And she especially loved him because he wasn't her **ex-husband**, who had problems with drink and work, and who was sleeping with his secretary.

Will went out with Angie for six weeks, but there were some things that he was beginning to find difficult. Once he booked tickets for the opening night of a new film, but Angie was half an hour late because she couldn't get a babysitter. And when they spent the night together, it always had to be at her place and she didn't have a video machine or many CDs.

But just when Will was thinking about ending the relationship, Angie decided to finish it.

ex-husband, ex-wife /ˌeks ˈhʌzbənd, ˌeks ˈwaɪf/ (n) the man or woman that you were married to but are not married to now

8

'Will, I'm so sorry, but I'm not sure this is working. It's not your fault. You've been great. It's me. Well, my situation, **anyway**. I've met you at the wrong time of my life and I'm not ready for a serious new relationship.'

It really was very strange, Will thought. Angie had believed he was serious about her, and he hadn't been serious at all. Now she was starting to cry. He had never before watched a woman cry without feeling responsible, and he was rather enjoying the experience.

'You don't have to be sorry for anything. Really.'

Of all the evenings he had spent with Angie, he loved the last one the best. The relationship had been perfect, and had finished in a perfect way too. Usually when his relationships with women ended, he felt guilty, but this time he had nothing to feel guilty about.

anyway /ˈeniweɪ/ (adv) a word used when you add a statement to explain or support what you have just said

Will knew then that there would be other women like Angie – bright, attractive single mothers, thousands of them all over London – and he knew he had a lot to offer them. He could sleep with them, make them feel better about themselves, be a parent for a limited time, and walk away without feeling guilty. What more could a man want?

◆

One Monday morning Marcus's mum started crying before breakfast, and it frightened him. Morning crying was something new, and it was a bad, bad sign. It meant that it could now start at any time of the day without warning.

When he went into the kitchen, she was sitting at the kitchen table in her night clothes, a half-eaten piece of toast on her plate, her eyes red from crying.

Marcus never said anything when she cried. He didn't know what to say. He didn't understand why she did it, and because he didn't understand, he couldn't help. So he stood there staring at her with his mouth open.

'Do you want some tea?' she asked him in a sad little voice.

'Yes. Please.' He made some toast, drank his tea and picked up his bag. Then he gave his mother a kiss and went out. Neither of them said a word. What else could he do?

On his way to school, he tried to work out what was wrong with her. What could be wrong that he didn't know about? He didn't think it was money problems. She had a job – she was a music teacher – so they weren't poor, although they weren't rich either. But they had enough money for the flat, and for food, and for holidays once a year, and even for occasional computer games.

What else made you cry? Death? But he'd know if anybody important had died. He'd seen all his relatives – his grandparents, his uncle Tom and uncle Tom's family – at a party the week before, and they'd all been fine. Was it about men? He knew his mum wanted a boyfriend because she joked about it sometimes. But if she joked about it, why should she suddenly start crying about it?

So what else was there? He tried to remember the other things that people cried about on TV programmes. Prison? An unwanted baby?

But Marcus had forgotten about his mum's problems by the time he was inside the school gates. He had his own problems to think about. A group of kids usually **bullied** him on his way across the playground. Today, though, they were at the other end, so he reached his classroom without difficulty.

His friends Nicky and Mark were already there, playing a game on Mark's Gameboy. He went over to them.

'All right?'

Nicky said hello, but Mark was too busy to notice him.

Marcus tried to watch the game, but he couldn't see the Gameboy very well, so he sat on a desk, waiting for them to finish. But when they finished, they started another game; they didn't offer him a game or put the Gameboy away. Marcus felt he was being shut out, and he didn't know what he'd done wrong.

'Are you going to the computer room at lunchtime?' he asked. That was how he knew Nicky and Mark – through the computer club. It was a stupid question because they always went to the computer room. It was the only place where they would be safe from the other kids.

'Don't know,' replied Nicky after a time. 'What do you think, Mark?'

'Don't know,' said Mark. 'Probably.'

---

bully /'bʊli/ (v) to frighten someone or say that you will hurt them, especially if they are smaller or younger than you

They weren't real friends – not like the friends he'd had in Cambridge – but he could talk to them because they were all different from the other kids in the class. All three of them wore glasses, none of them was interested in clothes and they all liked computer games.

Two older boys came and stood in the doorway. 'Give us a song,' they said to Marcus.

Marcus didn't know these boys, but they'd probably heard about him singing in the English class. Mark and Nicky started to move away, leaving him alone. Then the older boys started insulting Mark and Nicky, and making jokes about girls and sex. Mark turned the Gameboy off, and all three of them stood waiting for the boys to get bored and go away. Marcus tried to play a game inside his head, listing different kinds of chocolate.

At last the two older boys left. The three of them didn't say anything for a time. Then Nicky looked at Mark, and Mark looked at Nicky, and finally Mark spoke.

'Marcus, we don't want you with us.'

'Oh,' said Marcus. 'Why not?'

'Because of them.'

'They're not my problem.'

'Yes, they are,' said Mark. We never got into trouble with anyone before we knew you, and now we have problems every day.'

Marcus understood. They would be better without him. But he had nowhere else to go.

◆

Will was looking for ways to meet single mums like Angie, but he didn't know where to find them. Where did single mums go and how could he get their phone numbers? Then he had a wonderful idea. He would pretend to be a single father and join a single parents' group. So he invented a two-year-old son called Ned.

'I'm a single father. I have a two-year-old son. I'm a single father. I have a two-year-old son,' he told himself.

But he couldn't actually believe it. He didn't feel like a parent. He was too young, too old, too stupid, too intelligent, too cool, too impatient, too selfish, too careless, too careful. When he looked in the mirror, he couldn't see a dad, especially a single dad.

He telephoned a single parents' group called SPAT (Single Parents – Alone Together) and spoke to a woman called Frances. SPAT met on the first Thursday of each month in a local adult learning centre, and Frances invited Will to the next meeting. He was very worried that he'd get something wrong, like the name of his imaginary son – he couldn't stop thinking of him as Ted, not Ned.

The centre was a **depress**ing place with lots of classrooms. Will listened for the sounds of a party but he couldn't hear anything. Finally, he noticed a small piece of paper on a classroom door with the word SPAT! on it.

There was only one woman in the room. She was taking bottles – of white wine, beer and water – out of a box and putting them on a table in the centre of the room. All the other tables and chairs had been pushed to the back of the room. It was the most depressing place for a party that Will had ever seen.

'Have I come to the right place?' he asked the woman. She had a sharp nose and a bright red face.

'SPAT? Come in. Are you Will? I'm Frances.'

Will smiled and shook her hand.

'I'm sorry there's nobody else here yet,' she said. 'A lot of people are late because of problems with babysitters.'

'Of course,' said Will. He was wrong to come on time, he thought. He should pretend to have babysitting problems too. But then the other members of SPAT began to arrive, all women in their thirties, and Frances introduced him to each of them. The most attractive was a tall, blonde, nervous-looking woman. After she came into the room, he stopped looking at anybody else.

'Hello,' he said. 'I'm Will. I'm new and I don't know anybody.'

'Hello, Will. I'm Suzie. I'm old and I know everybody.'

He laughed. She laughed. He spent most of the evening with her. She talked a lot and he listened. He was very happy to listen because he didn't want to talk about Ned. Suzie had been married to a man called Dan, who had left her the day before she gave birth to her daughter Megan.

Suzie told him about the other women in the room. It was the same story – their husbands had all left them with children to look after. Will began to feel very depressed about being a man. How could men behave so badly?

'I'm sorry,' said Suzie at last. 'I haven't asked you anything about yourself. Did your wife leave you?'

'Well ... er ... yes.'

'And does she see Ned?'

'Sometimes. She's not very interested in him.' He was beginning to feel better; he could show her that women could behave badly too. He was acting, yes, but he was doing it well, just like Robert De Niro.

'How does Ned feel about that?' asked Suzie.

depress /dɪˈpres/ (v) to make someone feel very sad and without hope for the future

'Oh ... he's a good little boy,' said Will. 'Very brave.'

To his surprise, he was beginning to feel quite upset. Suzie put a hand on his arm. 'She likes me,' Will thought. 'Great!'

◆

Some parts of Marcus's life continued normally. He went to his dad's in Cambridge for the weekend and watched a lot of TV. On the Sunday he and his dad, and Lindsey, his dad's girlfriend, went to Lindsey's mum's house. Lindsey's mum lived by the sea, and they went for a long walk on the beach.

Marcus liked Lindsey's mum. He liked Lindsey too. Even his mum liked Lindsey. Marcus felt better after the weekend in Cambridge. He had a good time with everybody and nobody seemed to think he was weird.

But the day after he got back, he came home from school and found his mum lying on the floor with a coat over her.

'Didn't you go to work today?'

'This morning. I was sick this afternoon.'

'What kind of sick?' asked Marcus.

She didn't reply, and Marcus felt angry. He was only a kid and things couldn't continue like this. He was having an awful time at school and an awful time at home, and school and home were almost the only places he knew. So someone was going to have to help him, and that person had to be his mum. She had to do something about it. He was only a kid, and she was his mum, and if he felt bad it was her job to stop him feeling bad.

'What kind of sick?' he asked again in a rough voice.

She began to cry and Marcus felt frightened.

'You've got to stop this.'

'I can't.'

'You've got to. If you can't look after me, then you'll have to find someone who can.'

His mum turned over on her stomach and looked at him. 'How can you say I don't look after you?'

'Because you don't. You make my meals and I could do that. The rest of the time, you just cry. That's ... that's no good. That's no good to me.'

She cried even more then. Marcus went upstairs and played a computer game, but when he came downstairs again, she had got up and was cooking supper.

'You're going to a **picnic** on Saturday,' she said suddenly.

'A picnic? Where?'

'In Regent's Park.'

---

picnic /'pɪknɪk/ (n) a meal outdoors, away from your house, with food that you have taken with you

'Who with?'

'Suzie.'

'Not that SPAT crowd.'

'Yes, that SPAT crowd.'

'I hate them.' When Marcus and his mum had first moved to London, they had gone to a SPAT summer party in someone's garden. It had been full of horrible little kids, all about ten years younger than Marcus.

'Are you going?' he asked.

'No. I need a rest. You told me to find someone to look after you. So that's what I'm doing. Suzie's better at it than I am.'

Suzie was Fiona's best friend; they'd known each other since their schooldays. She was nice and Marcus liked her a lot. But he didn't want to go to a SPAT picnic.

'I can stay here. I'll keep out of your way. I can sit in my room all day, playing games.'

'I want you to get out. Do something normal. We're not doing each other any good.'

Marcus was shocked. What did she mean, they weren't doing *each other* any good? She wasn't doing *him* any good, but what had he done to *her*? He couldn't think of anything. He felt like crying too.

2.1 Were you right?

Look back at your notes in Activity 1.2 on page iv. Then decide whether these sentences are right (✓) or wrong (✗).

1 ☐ Will likes children.
3 ☐ The children at school are unkind to Marcus.
2 ☐ Marcus likes school.
4 ☐ Marcus is worried about his mother.

2.2 What more did you learn?

1 Circle the correct words.

a Will *has / hasn't got* a job.

b Marcus and Fiona live in *London / Cambridge.*

c Marcus's dad lives in *London / Cambridge.*

d Will *wants / doesn't want* to meet single mothers.

e Suzie *believes / doesn't believe* that Will has a son called Ned.

2 Answer the questions with the names in the box.

| Angie | Fiona | Marcus | Mark | Suzie | Will |

a Who has a strange haircut? ....

b Who has lots of girlfriends? ....

c Who doesn't like computer games? ....

d Who ends a relationship with Will? ....

e Who tells Marcus to go away? ....

f Who meets Will at SPAT? ....

3 Complete this poster for SPAT.

PARENTS ⬭ TOGETHER

TIRED?
LONELY?
IN NEED OF NEW FRIENDS?
YOU are not alone.

Join us in the ⬭ learning centre at 8pm on the first ⬭ of each month.

2.3 Language in use

1 Look at the sentences in the box, and then at the sentences below. What happened first (1)? What happened second (2)?

> **1** Will didn't need to work for money because in 1938 his father **had written** a very successful Christmas song.
>
> **2** Before moving to London, they **had lived** in Cambridge.
>
> **3** Marcus **had forgotten** about his mum's problems by the time he was inside the school gates.

1 a Will didn't need to work. ....

   b Will's father wrote a song. ....

2 a Marcus and Fiona moved to London. ....

   b Marcus and Fiona lived in Cambridge. ....

3 a Marcus forgot about his mum's problems. ....

   b Marcus was inside the school gates. ....

2 Complete the sentences with the verbs in the box.

> didn't want   were   had been   had enjoyed   had gone
> moved   had separated   had sung   laughed   was

1 Before their children .... *were* .... born, John and Christine .... *had gone* .... out to nightclubs with Will.

2 Will .... seeing his friends but now he .... to visit them.

3 Marcus's parents .... before Marcus .... to London.

4 Marcus's school in Cambridge .... OK, but his new school .... horrible.

5 The other kids .... at Marcus because he .... a song in class.

2.4 What happens next?

Look at the pictures in Chapters 3 and 4. Discuss what you think will happen in this part of the story.

The Dead Duck Day

'Fiona! How could you do this?' Suzie screamed.
'You've got a kid! How could you do this?'

Will wanted to go to the SPAT picnic in Regent's Park because Suzie was going. But he knew that Suzie would expect Ned to be there too, so he had to invent a reason why Ned couldn't go. He telephoned Suzie on the morning of the picnic and told her that his ex-wife had taken Ned out.

'But that's terrible, Will,' said Suzie. 'You can't let her change your plans like that.'

'I know, I know,' he said. 'And she's taken my car too. Can I go with you to Regent's Park?'

'Yes, of course,' replied Suzie. 'I'm bringing a twelve-year-old kid too – Marcus, my friend Fiona's son. She's asked me to look after him for the day.'

All the way to the park Suzie talked about Will's ex-wife. She was very angry about Paula's behaviour. Had he called her Paula? Will couldn't remember. Things were getting rather complicated, he thought. How much longer could he

continue pretending? And how could he ever invite Suzie round to his flat? There were no toys there, and he didn't even have two bedrooms.

They walked through the park to the lake. Suzie was pushing her daughter, Megan, in a pushchair, and Marcus was walking beside them. Will thought Marcus was a weird kid. He had a very strange haircut and odd clothes.

'I don't even know what you do,' said Suzie.

'Nothing.' He usually invented a job, but he had told enough lies. He had to give Suzie something that was real.

'Oh. Well, what did you do before?'

'Nothing.'

'You've never worked?'

'Well, only for a day or two. My dad wrote a famous song, and I live from the royalties.'

'Michael Jackson makes £60 million an hour,' said the weird kid. 'How much do you make?'

'Marcus!' said Suzie. 'So what's this song, Will?'

Will told them. He hated telling people because the title sounded so silly.

'Really?' Suzie and Marcus both started singing the same part of the song. People always did this, and he hated that too.

'But haven't you ever wanted to work?' asked Suzie.

'Oh, yes, sometimes, but I never seem to do anything about it.' It was true. Every day for the last eighteen years he had got up in the morning thinking about finding a job. But by the evening he had lost interest.

He decided to talk to Marcus. If he made friends with Marcus, Suzie would think he was a nice guy.

'So, Marcus,' he said, 'who's your favourite footballer?'

'I hate football.'

'Right,' said Will. 'Well, who's your favourite singer?'

'Are you getting these questions out of a book?' asked Marcus.

Suzie laughed, and Will's face turned red.

'No,' he said. 'I'm just interested.'

'OK,' said Marcus. 'Well, it's Joni Mitchell.'

'Really?' said Will in surprise. 'Does everyone in your school listen to Joni Mitchell?'

'Most people.'

Will was confused. He read a lot of modern music magazines, but none of them had said anything about Joni Mitchell's new popularity.

Marcus turned away, so Will began to talk to Suzie.

'Do you often have to look after him?' he asked.

'Not often. But Fiona, his mum, isn't feeling very well.'

'She's going crazy,' said Marcus calmly. 'Cries all the time. Doesn't go to work.'

'She isn't crazy. She just needs a rest.'

They could see the SPAT crowd of mothers and children sitting by the lake in front of them. The mothers were pouring juice into cups, and the children were eating sandwiches.

Will played with the children for most of the afternoon. He kept away from the adults sitting on blankets under a tree because he didn't want to have to answer difficult questions about Ned. He kept away from Marcus too. Marcus was walking round the lake, throwing bits of his sandwich at the **ducks**.

Later, Suzie came to talk to him. 'You miss him, don't you?'

'Who?' He meant it; he had no idea what she was talking about. But then he remembered about Ned. 'I'll see him later.'

'What's he like?' asked Suzie.

duck /dʌk/ (n) a common water bird with short legs

'Oh ... Nice. He's a really nice boy.'

Before Suzie could ask more questions, Marcus ran over to them. He seemed very nervous and upset.

'I think I've killed a duck,' he said.

Will, Suzie, Marcus and Megan stood on the path by the edge of the lake, staring at the duck's dead body in the water.

'What happened, Marcus?' Will asked.

'I don't know. I was just throwing a piece of my sandwich at it. I didn't mean to kill it.'

'What's that in the water next to it? Is that the bread you threw at it?'

'Yes,' said Marcus. He didn't like Will much, so he didn't want to answer his questions.

'That's not a sandwich, that's a loaf,' said Will. 'I'm not surprised the duck was killed.'

'Perhaps I didn't kill it,' said Marcus. 'Perhaps it died because it was ill.'

Nobody said anything.

They were all staring so hard at the scene of the crime that they didn't notice the park-keeper standing next to them. Marcus felt very frightened. He would be in big trouble now.

'One of your ducks has died,' said Will. He made it sound like the saddest thing he'd ever seen. Marcus looked up at him. Maybe Will wasn't such a bad guy.

'I was told it was your boy's fault,' said the park-keeper. 'It's a crime to kill a duck, you know.'

'Are you suggesting that Marcus killed this duck? Marcus *loves* ducks, don't you, Marcus?'

'Yes,' said Marcus. 'They're my favourite animal. I mean, my favourite bird.' This was rubbish, because he hated all animals, but he thought it helped.

'I was told he was throwing enormous loaves at it.'

'No,' said Will. 'He was throwing bread at the duck's body. He wanted to sink it because the sight of a dead bird was upsetting my friend's little girl, Megan.'

There was a silence. At last the park-keeper spoke.

'Well, I'll have to go into the water and get it,' he said.

Marcus felt much better. He wouldn't have to go to prison.

They were walking back to the rest of the SPAT group when suddenly a strange thing happened. Marcus saw – or thought he saw – his mum. She was standing on the path in front of them and she was smiling. But when he looked again, she wasn't there.

Usually when Suzie took Marcus home after a day out, she left him outside his flat and waited until he got inside. But today she parked the car and lifted Megan out in her car seat. She was never able to explain why she had done this. Will wasn't invited, but he followed them in.

Marcus put the key in the door of the flat and opened it, and a new part of his life began, without any warning at all.

His mum was half on and half off the sofa. Her face was white, and there was a pool of sick on the carpet and an empty pill bottle beside her.

He couldn't speak. He didn't know what to say. He didn't cry either – the situation was much too serious for that, so he just stood there. But Suzie dropped the car seat and ran over to his mum and started screaming at her and shaking her. Marcus was confused. Why was Suzie so angry with someone who wasn't very well?

Suzie shouted at Will to call for an ambulance, and told Marcus to make some black coffee. His mum was moving now and making a terrible noise that Marcus had never heard before and never wanted to hear again.

'Fiona! How could you do this?' Suzie screamed. 'You've got a kid! How could you do this?'

Suddenly Marcus understood that his mum had tried to kill herself. He had seen some shocking things, mostly on videos at other people's houses, but they hadn't frightened him because they weren't real life. This situation with his mum was different because it was very real. There wasn't anything shocking in the room, and he could see that his mum wasn't dead. But it was the most frightening thing he'd ever seen, and he knew he'd never forget it.

When the ambulance arrived and Fiona was taken to hospital, the ambulance men didn't want to take Marcus and Megan too. So Suzie went to the hospital with Fiona, and Will drove Marcus and Megan there in Suzie's car.

When they arrived at the hospital, Fiona had already been taken away.

'What's happening?' asked Will. He was finding the whole experience very interesting – almost enjoyable.

'I don't know. They're **pump**ing her stomach or something. She was talking a little in the ambulance. She was asking about you, Marcus.'

'That's nice of her.'

Suzie tried to put her arms round him. 'Listen, Marcus,' she said. 'This isn't about you. You know that, don't you? I mean, you're not the reason she ... you're not the reason she's here.'

'How do you know?' He pushed Suzie away and went to get a drink from a machine.

pump /pʌmp/ (v) to remove liquid from somewhere, using special equipment

'What can you tell a kid whose mother has just tried to kill herself?' Will asked. He really wanted to know.

'I don't know,' said Suzie worriedly. 'But we'll have to think of something.'

They waited in the hospital for a long time. Megan went to sleep and Marcus ate a lot of sweets and chocolate from the machine. None of them talked much. At last a woman came over to see them – not a nurse or a doctor, but somebody official.

'Hello. Did you come in with Fiona Brewer?'

'Yes. I'm her friend Suzie, and this is Will, and this is Fiona's son Marcus.'

'Right. We're keeping Fiona here for the night. Is there somewhere Marcus could go?'

'He can stay with me tonight,' said Suzie.

She put Megan back into the car seat and they made their way out to the car park.

'I'll see you soon,' said Will. 'I'll call you.'

'I hope things are OK with Ned and Paula,' Suzie said.

For a moment Will didn't know who she meant. Ned and Paula, Ned and Paula ...? Ah, yes – his ex-wife and son.

'Oh, it'll be fine. Thanks.' He said goodbye and went to find a taxi. It had been a very interesting experience, but he wouldn't want to repeat it every night.

CHAPTER 4

Marcus's Plan

It would feel like the beginning of a different, better time. But that time wouldn't last for ever. Marcus knew that, for him, things would never be the same again.

The next day Suzie took Marcus home and left him while she went to get Fiona from the hospital. He was just tidying the kitchen, as Suzie had told him to do, when he saw a note on the kitchen table. He picked it up and sat down.

Dear Marcus,
A big part of me knows that I'm doing a wrong, stupid, selfish, unkind thing. But unfortunately that's not the part that has control of me now. None of this is about you. I've loved being your mum, always, although I've found it difficult sometimes. And I don't know why it isn't enough for me, but it isn't. I just feel very tired, and there doesn't seem to be anything to look forward to. Things will be better for you than they were before. Really. You can go to your dad's, or Suzie has always said she'd look after you. Love you,
Mum

Marcus was still sitting at the kitchen table when his mum came back from the hospital with Suzie and Megan. She could see immediately what he'd found.

'I'm sorry, Marcus. I'd forgotten about the note.'

'You forgot? You forgot you wrote a letter about killing yourself?'

'Well, I didn't think I'd ever have to remember it, did I?' She laughed at that. She actually laughed. That was his mother. When she wasn't crying at breakfast, she was laughing about killing herself.

'It was stupid of me to leave Marcus here before I went to get you,' said Suzie. 'I wasn't thinking.'

'Suzie, none of this is your fault. But maybe Marcus and I ought to have a little talk alone.'

'Of course,' said Suzie. She gave Marcus a kiss. 'She's fine,' she whispered, loud enough for his mum to hear. 'Don't worry about her.'

When Suzie had gone, Fiona made tea and sat down at the table with Marcus.

'Are you angry with me?'

'What do you think?'

'Because of the letter?'

'Because of the letter, because of what you did, everything.'

'I can understand that. I don't feel the same as I did on Saturday, if that's any help.'

'So your problems have all just gone away?'

'No, but ... at the moment I feel better.'

'At the moment's no good to me,' said Marcus. 'I can see that you're better at the moment. You've just made tea. But what happens when I go back to school? I can't be here to watch you all the time.'

'No, I know. But we've got to look after each other.'

Marcus was no longer interested in what his mum said; the important thing was what she did, or what she was going to do. She wasn't going to try and kill herself again today. She'd drink her tea, and tonight they'd watch TV, and it would feel like the beginning of a different, better time. But that time wouldn't last for ever. Marcus knew that, for him, things would never be the same again.

Two people in a family weren't enough. He'd always thought that two was a good number, and that he'd hate to live in a family of three or four or five. But now he could see that if there were lots of people in a family, and one of them died, you wouldn't be left on your own. But how could he make his family grow? He was going to have to find a way.

◆

Will kept thinking about Marcus and Fiona. There wasn't much else happening in his life, so he had a lot of time to think about them. He had a strange thought: perhaps he should try and help them. He telephoned Suzie.

'I was wondering how Marcus and Fiona are,' he said.

'Not too bad, I think. She hasn't gone back to work, but Marcus went to school today.'

'Listen, do you think there's any way I could help? Perhaps I could take Marcus out?'

'Would you like to?' said Suzie. 'I could ask Fiona.'

'Thanks,' said Will. 'And it would be nice to see you and Megan again soon.'

'Yes,' said Suzie. 'I'm looking forward to meeting Ned.'

Will bought *Time Out*, a magazine with information about events in London. He was looking for something that a twelve-year-old boy might like to do on a Saturday. He tried to remember what he liked doing at Marcus's age, but he couldn't. Then the telephone rang.

'Hi, Will. It's Marcus.'

'Hi, Marcus.'

'Suzie said you want to take me out for the day on Saturday. I'll come if my mum can come too.'

'What?'

'I'll come if my mum can come too. And she hasn't got any money, so we'll either have to go somewhere cheap, or you'll have to pay for us.'

'Well ... wouldn't it be better with just you and me? Your mum could stay at home and have a rest.'

Suddenly Will remembered last Saturday. They had left Fiona at home to rest, and she had tried to kill herself.

'I'm sorry, Marcus,' he said quickly. 'I wasn't thinking. Of course your mum can come too. That would be great.'

'We haven't got a car. You'll have to bring yours. And you can bring your little boy if you like.'

He laughed. 'Thanks.'

'That's OK,' said Marcus generously.

'He'll be with his mum again on Saturday.'

'Fine. Come round at about half past twelve. You remember where we live. Flat 2, 31 Craysfield Road, Islington, London N1 2SF.'

'Right,' said Will. 'See you then.'

◆

Marcus wasn't really worried about leaving his mum. She was still in a strange, calm mood. But he wanted her to come so that she and Will could meet, and after that, he thought, it should be easy. His mum was pretty, and Will seemed quite rich. They could go and live with him and his kid, and then there would be four of them, and four was twice as good as two. Then if one of them died, it wouldn't matter so much.

Marcus wasn't even sure whether he liked Will or not, but it didn't matter. He could see that Will wasn't bad, or drunk, or violent, so he would be OK. And Marcus knew a little about Will. One day on his way home from school, he had seen Will out shopping and had followed him home like a private detective.

He hadn't really found out much about him except where he lived. But Will seemed to live alone – no girlfriend, no wife, no little boy. Perhaps the little boy was with his girlfriend at home? But if Will had a girlfriend, why was he trying to get friendly with Suzie?

When Will arrived on Saturday, his mum was looking good, Marcus thought. She was wearing her best trousers and a hairy jumper, and she was wearing make-up for the first time since the hospital, and a pair of brightly coloured earrings from Zimbabwe.

'Thanks for everything you did last weekend,' she said. 'I'm very grateful.'

'It was a pleasure. I hope you're feeling ... I hope you've ...'

'My stomach's fine. I suppose I must still be a bit crazy, though. That sort of thing doesn't get better quickly, does it?'

Will looked shocked, but she just laughed. Marcus hated it when she made jokes to people who didn't know her well.

Will took them to a restaurant called Twenty-Eight. After they had ordered their food, Marcus hoped that Will and his mum would start talking. But they seemed to be finding it difficult to start a conversation, so he had to help them.

'Don't just sit there,' he said. 'Talk to each other.'

Both Will and Fiona looked at him.

'What do you want us to talk about?' asked Will.

'Anything. Politics. Films. Murders. I don't care.'

'I'm not sure that's how conversation happens,' said his mother.

Marcus started asking questions to make them talk, but he wasn't very successful.

'Leave us alone, Marcus. You're making it more difficult, not easier,' said Fiona. 'We'll start talking soon.'

Then Will asked questions about Marcus's dad, and soon they were talking about relationships. They were talking so much that they didn't notice when the food arrived. Marcus ate his lunch happily. Would they move into Will's place, he wondered, or buy somewhere new?

◆

Will knew that Fiona wasn't his type of woman. She didn't look the way he wanted women to look. He didn't think looks were important to her at all. Why didn't she get a good haircut and wear nice clothes? And she was just too strange. He could see now why Marcus was so weird. She believed in things that Will didn't care about, like being a **vegetarian**.

Will still wanted to help them. One evening he was invited to supper at their flat. He didn't like the food very much – something vegetarian with peas and rice and tinned tomatoes – but he quite enjoyed the conversation. Fiona told him about her job as a music teacher and they talked about his dad's song. But later Fiona sat down at the piano and started to sing.

She wasn't a bad singer, but Will was very embarrassed. She sang old pop songs from the sixties, and she sang them with deep feeling; she even closed her eyes. Then Marcus began to sing too, in the same way, and they made Will sing with them. It was awful.

Will could see that he'd made a big mistake about Marcus and Fiona. He couldn't do anything to help people like them. They were too weird and they felt too deeply about things. Will didn't feel deeply about anything. He couldn't imagine wanting to kill himself. He just wanted to live a long life without any problems.

Fiona called Will and left a message on his answer machine, but he didn't call her back. He was trying to return to his old life. He went shopping for CDs and clothes, he played a bit of tennis, he went to the pub and to see films with friends. Then, one afternoon, the doorbell rang. It was Marcus.

'I've come to see you,' he said.

'Oh. Right. Come in.'

vegetarian /ˌvedʒəˈteəriən/ (n/adj) someone who does not eat meat or fish

Marcus marched into the sitting room, sat down on the sofa and looked round. 'You haven't got a kid, have you?'

'Well ...' began Will.

Marcus got up and walked around the flat. 'Where's your toilet?' he asked.

'It's just down the hall.'

When Marcus was gone, Will tried to think what he could say about Ned, but he couldn't think of anything.

'You've only got one bedroom,' said Marcus when he got back. 'You've got no children's toys in the bathroom, there are no toys in here ... You haven't even got any photos of him.'

'Is that your business?'

'No. But you've been lying to me, and my mum, and my mum's friend.'

'Who told you where I live?'

'I followed you here once.'

'Why don't you just go home, Marcus?'

'All right. But I'm going to tell my mum.'

Will couldn't think of any explanation to give Marcus except the **truth** – that he had invented a child so he could join a single parents' group and meet women. And the truth sounded much worse than he had ever intended.

'Listen, Will,' said Marcus. 'I won't say anything to my mum if you go out with her.'

'Why do you want your mum to go out with someone like me?'

'I don't think you're too bad. I mean, you told lies, but you seem OK. She's sad, and I think she'd like a boyfriend.'

'Marcus, I can't go out with someone just because you want me to. I have to like the person too.'

'What's wrong with her?'

'Nothing's wrong with her, but ...'

'You want to go out with Suzie, don't you?'

'I don't want to talk about this with you.'

'I thought so.'

'I didn't say anything. I just said ... Listen, I really don't want to talk about this with you. Go home.'

'OK,' said Marcus. 'But I'll be back.'

When Will had joined SPAT, he'd imagined entering the world of single mothers and their sweet children. He hadn't imagined Marcus, and he hadn't expected anyone to break into *his* world. He was one of life's visitors; he didn't want to be visited.

truth /truːθ/ (n) the true facts about something

3.1 Were you right?

Think back to your discussion in Activity 2.4. Then look at the picture below and answer these questions.

1 Who are the ambulance men taking to hospital? Why?

....

....

2 Who are the other people in the picture? Where have they been?

....

....

3 What do they do next?

....

4 What happens the next day?

....

3.2 What more did you learn?

Match the beginnings of the sentences with the correct endings.

1 Fiona asks Suzie ☐   **a** and kills a duck.

2 Will goes to the picnic ☐   **b** to take Marcus out for the day.

3 Marcus throws a loaf of bread ☐   **c** from hospital the next day.

4 Fiona wants to die, ☐   **d** with Suzie, Megan and Marcus.

5 Marcus finds a letter ☐   **e** from his mum.

6 Fiona comes home ☐ c   **f** Fiona and Marcus.

7 Will wants to help ☐   **g** to go out with his mum.

8 Marcus wants Will ☐   **h** but she doesn't.

3.3 Language in use

Look at the sentences in the box. Then complete the sentences below with the correct form of the verb.

> If he **made** friends with Marcus, Suzie **would think** he was a nice guy.
>
> If one of them **died**, you **wouldn't be left** on your own.

1 If Marcus (not look) ......*didn't look*.... strange, the other kids (not laugh) ...*wouldn't laugh*... at him.

2 Marcus (not worry) .... about his mum if she (not cry) .... so much.

3 Suzie (not like) .... Will if she (know) .... he was telling lies.

4 There (be) .... more mess in Will's flat if he really (have) .... a child.

5 If Marcus (can find) .... a boyfriend for his mum, he (feel) .... better.

6 If there (be) .... more people in his family, Marcus (be) .... safer.

3.4 What happens next?

1 Look at the words in *italics* at the top of page 38. Tick (✓) the sentence that you think is correct.

   a ☐ Will has started having tea parties for Marcus and his school friends.

   b ☐ Marcus invites himself to Will's flat at tea time.

   c ☐ Marcus hasn't been to Will's flat - Fiona has imagined it.

2 Look at the words in *italics* at the top of page 45. Tick (✓) the sentence that you think is correct.

   a ☐ Marcus has changed schools.

   b ☐ Marcus has become a school hero.

   c ☐ Marcus has made a friend.

CHAPTER 5

New Trainers

'Why do you invite twelve-year-old boys round to tea-parties in your flat after school?' asked Fiona.

Marcus knew that he couldn't make Will go out with his mum if Will didn't want to. But he knew Will's secret now, so perhaps he could make him do something else. He started going round to Will's flat after school.

The first time, Will wasn't very pleased to see him. He stood in the doorway and didn't invite Marcus in.

'What?'

'I just thought I'd come round. What are you doing?'

'Watching *Countdown*.'

Marcus knew about *Countdown* – the most boring programme in the history of television. But he wanted to get inside Will's flat.

'I could watch it with you if you want. I really like it.'

Will looked at him for a time. 'All right. Come in.'

There were lots of interesting things in Will's flat – hundreds of CDs, records and cassettes. There were pictures from films on the wall, and black and white photos of people with musical instruments.

'Who are these people? And why are they on your wall?'

'They're musicians. And they're on my wall because I like their music and they're cool.'

'Why are they cool?'

'I don't know. Because they took drugs and died, probably.'

Marcus thought he wouldn't want pictures on his wall of people who took drugs and died. He'd want to forget all about that kind of thing, not look at it every day of his life.

Will made tea in the kitchen. Then they went back into the living room and sat down on the sofa.

'Do you like school?' Will asked.

'No. I hate it.'

'Why? Do the other kids bully you?'

Marcus looked at him. How did he know that?

'Not really. Just a couple of kids.'

'What do they do to you?'

'Nothing really. Just, you know, say things about my hair and glasses. And my singing. Sometimes ... I sing without noticing.' Will laughed. 'It's not funny.'

'I'm sorry. But you could do something about your hair. You could have it cut in the way you want it.'

'This is how I want it.'

'Why do you want your hair like that?'

'Because that's how it grows, and I hate going to the hairdresser.'

'I can see that. How often do you go?'

'Never. My mum cuts it.'

'Your mum? How old are you? Twelve? You're old enough to get your hair cut yourself. You could get married in four years' time. Will you let your mum cut your hair then?'

Marcus didn't think he'd be married in four years' time, but he understood what Will was telling him and knew that Will was right. But there was another way of looking at the situation. If his mum was going to cut his hair in four years' time, then she would still be alive.

Marcus visited Will a lot that autumn, and by about the third or fourth visit he felt that Will was getting used to him. They didn't talk about much at first, but one day Will said, 'How's the situation at home?' for no reason that Marcus could understand.

'You mean my mum?'

'Yes.'

'She's all right, thanks.'

Marcus had never talked about it, and he'd never said how he felt. But what he felt, all the time, every day, was a horrible fear. This was the main reason why he came round to Will's after school. Every time he climbed the stairs at home he remembered the Dead Duck Day. When he saw his mum watching the news or eating or preparing work on the dining table, he wanted to cry, or be sick or something. But he couldn't talk about it.

'Are you still worried about her?'

'A bit, when I think about it.'

'How often do you think about it?'

'I don't know.' He thought about it all the time, all the time, all the time. Could he say that to Will? He didn't know. He couldn't say it to his mum, or to his dad, or to Suzie. They would all be too worried about him. He just wanted a promise from someone, anyone, that it wouldn't happen again, ever, and no one could do that.

Will was wishing that he hadn't asked Marcus about Fiona, because it was clear that the boy was very upset. Will wasn't used to coping with people with real-life problems. He liked watching people's problems on TV, but he'd never had anyone with problems on his sofa before.

Sometimes they managed conversations about other things, like Marcus's dad.

'Do you see your dad often?'

'Quite often. Some weekends. He's got a girlfriend called Lindsey. She's nice.'

'Would you like to see him more than you do?'

'No.'

'Well, that's all right, then.'

The next week, while Will was watching *Countdown* as usual, he was interrupted by a long, urgent ring on the doorbell. He got up off the sofa and opened the door. Marcus was standing on the doorstep, and two ugly-looking boys were throwing hard sweets at him. Some sweets hit Will.

'What do you think you're doing?' He couldn't remember the last time he had been so angry.

The boys ran away and Will went back into the flat. Marcus was sitting on the sofa watching *Countdown*.

'Who were they?'

'I don't know their names,' said Marcus, his eyes on the TV. 'They're in the class two years above me at school.'

'Marcus, does this happen often?'

'Well, they've never thrown sweets at me before.'

'I'm not talking about the sweets. I'm talking about older kids bullying you.'

'Oh, yes. Not those two ...'

'No, OK, not those two. But others like them.'

'Yes. Lots.'

'Right. That's what I've been trying to find out. Your problem is, Marcus, that you look different from other kids. That's why they notice you. You need to look more like them. You need the same clothes and haircut and glasses as everyone else. You can be as weird as you want on the inside. Just do something about the outside.'

Will took Marcus shopping in Holloway Road and bought him a pair of expensive Adidas **trainers**. Marcus thought they were cool, and Will was pleased. He couldn't remember feeling as good as this before. He had made an unhappy boy happy, and there hadn't been any advantage in it for him at all. He didn't even want to sleep with the boy's mother.

But the next day Marcus's new trainers were stolen. He came home from school wearing only a pair of black socks.

'Where are your shoes?' Fiona screamed. She hadn't noticed that he had been wearing new trainers.

'Stolen.'

'Stolen? Why would anyone want to steal your shoes?'

'Because ...' He was going to have to tell her the truth, although he knew the truth would lead to a lot of questions. 'Because they were nice ones. They were new Adidas trainers. Will bought them for me.'

'Will who? Will, the guy who took us to lunch?'

'Yes. The guy from SPAT. He's become my friend.'

'He's become your friend?'

Marcus was right – his mum had lots of questions, but she asked them in a very boring way. She just repeated the last thing he said, made it into a question and shouted.

'I go round to his flat after school.'

'YOU GO ROUND TO HIS FLAT AFTER SCHOOL?'

'Well, you see, he doesn't really have a kid.'

'HE DOESN'T REALLY HAVE A KID?'

When the questions had finished, he was in a lot of trouble, although probably not as much trouble as Will. Marcus put his old shoes back on, and then he and his mother went straight to Will's flat. Will opened the door and Fiona immediately started shouting at him about SPAT and his imaginary son.

---

trainers /ˈtreɪnəz/ (n pl) sports shoes, especially running shoes, that are also worn in everyday life

At first Will looked embarrassed – he had no answers to her questions, so he stood there staring at the floor. But as it continued, he started to get angry too.

'Why do you invite twelve-year-old boys round to tea-parties in your flat after school?' asked Fiona.

Will looked at her. 'Are you suggesting what I think you're suggesting?' He went red in the face and started shouting very loudly. 'Your son invites himself round here. Sometimes he's followed by other kids who attack him. I could leave him outside, but I let him in for his own safety. I won't do it again. Now, if you've finished, you can both get out of here.'

'I haven't finished yet, actually. Why did you buy him a pair of expensive trainers?'

'Because ... because *look* at him.'

'What's wrong with him?'

Will looked at her. 'You really don't know, do you? Marcus is being eaten alive at school by the other kids. He gets bullied every day.'

'Marcus is doing fine,' his mother said.

Marcus couldn't believe she'd said that. He wasn't doing fine; his mum was being blind and stupid and crazy.

'You're joking,' said Will.

'I know he's taking some time to get used to his new school, but ...'

Will laughed. 'Oh, yes. And after a couple of weeks he'll be OK? When they've stopped stealing his shoes and following him home from school, everything will be great.'

That was wrong. They were all mad. 'I don't think so,' said Marcus. 'It's going to take more than a couple of weeks.'

'It's OK, I know,' said Will. 'I was joking.'

Marcus didn't think there was much to joke about in the situation. But he was very pleased that Will understood what was happening to him at school. He'd only known Will for a short time, and he'd known his mother all his life. So why could Will understand, and his mother couldn't? But now his mother understood too, because Will had told her.

'You're not going to Will's again,' Fiona said to Marcus on the bus on the way home. 'If you've got anything to say, you say it to me. If you need new clothes, I'll get them.'

'But you don't know what I need. *I* don't know what I need. Only Will knows. He knows what kids wear.'

'We don't need that kind of person. We're doing all right our way. Marcus, I've been your mother for twelve years. I do know what I'm doing.'

Marcus didn't think either of them was doing all right. He wondered if his mother had a kind of plan for him. In the next few days he began to notice the way she talked to him. He was interested in everything she said about what he should watch on TV or listen to or read or eat.

She had always said it was important to talk about things, and that she wanted him to think for himself. They had often discussed what was bad about fashion and modern pop music and computer games. But if she didn't like what he said, she argued with him until he agreed with her. But he hadn't agreed, really; he'd just lost the argument.

'I've been thinking for myself,' he said, 'and I want to go round to Will's flat after school.'

'No. He's a rich guy who doesn't work, who tells lies, and who ...'

'He understands about school. He bought me those trainers. He knows things.' He was getting annoyed. 'I'm thinking for myself and ... it doesn't work. You always win.'

'Marcus, it's not enough to tell me you're thinking for yourself. You've got to show me too. Give me a good reason why you want to go round to Will's.'

Marcus gave her a reason. It wasn't the right reason, and he felt bad saying it because it made her cry. But it was a good reason and he won the argument.

'Because I need a father.'

CHAPTER 6

Ellie

*'OK, listen, everybody. I want you to meet Marcus.
He's the only other person in the whole school who likes Kurt Cobain.'*

Will hadn't seen Marcus for a week and hadn't thought about him much. He preferred watching *Countdown* alone, anyway. Then Fiona phoned.

'Marcus seems to think he needs an adult male in his life. Like a father. He talked about you.'

'Listen, Fiona, I definitely don't need a son in my life. Why doesn't he use his own father as a father?'

'His father lives in Cambridge. It's a long way.'

'You told me not to see Marcus again. Fine. I told you I didn't want to see Marcus again. And now you're telling me ... I don't understand.'

'Listen,' said Fiona. 'Can we meet tomorrow night for a drink to discuss all this?'

They met in a quiet pub. Will had never been alone with Fiona before. He didn't find her attractive and he certainly didn't want to sleep with her. But conversations with her were never dull.

'I've always been worried about Marcus not having a father around,' said Fiona. 'But he's always told me it didn't matter. Then, when I said I didn't want him to see you, he said he needed a father.'

'He said that because he wanted to win the argument. Never **trust** a human male when he talks about his feelings.'

'Really? Well, maybe it's best if he doesn't see you.'

'What do you want me to do if he rings the doorbell?'

'Don't let him in.'

'Right.'

Marcus was waiting for Fiona at home. He didn't like the idea of his mum talking to Will because he'd stopped believing that he and his mum and Will and Ned were going to live together in Will's flat. Ned didn't exist, and Will and Fiona didn't like each other very much.

When Fiona came back, he looked at her face to see if she was angry or depressed, but she seemed OK.

'Did you have a good time?'

'It was OK. But you're not going round there again. He's not going to answer the door. He told me.'

Marcus wasn't worried. He knew how loudly Will's doorbell rang inside the flat, and he knew he could ring it for a very long time.

◆

Fiona had made a complaint to the school about Marcus's new trainers being stolen, so he had to go and see the head teacher, Mrs Morrison. He was waiting outside her office when a girl called Ellie McCrae came and sat down next to him. Ellie was fifteen and she was famous in the school. She wore a lot of black eye make-up and cut her own hair, and she was always in trouble, usually for something serious.

They sat in silence for a time, then Marcus thought he'd try to talk to Ellie. His mum was always saying he should talk to people at school.

'Hello, Ellie.'

'How does a little boy like you know my name?'

'You're famous.' He knew this was a mistake immediately.

'What am I famous for?'

'Don't know.'

'Yes, you do. I'm famous because I'm always in trouble. Do you know what I'm in trouble for this time? It's this **sweatshirt**. They don't want me to wear it, and I don't want to take it off, so there's going to be an argument.'

trust /trʌst/ (v) to believe that someone will not lie to you or harm you
sweatshirt /'swet-ʃɜːt/ (n) a piece of clothing of thick, soft cotton that covers your upper body and arms

Marcus looked at Ellie's sweatshirt. It had a
picture on it of a guy with long blond hair, big eyes and half a beard.

'Who's that?' he asked politely.

'Don't you know? It's Kirk O'Bane.'

'Oh, yes.' Marcus had never heard of Kirk O'Bane, but that wasn't surprising
– he'd never heard of anybody. 'What does he do?'

'He's a footballer. He plays for Manchester United.'

'Does he?' Marcus thought that the guy on Ellie's sweatshirt looked more like
a singer than a footballer. Footballers weren't sad, usually, and this man looked sad.

Just then Mrs Morrison's door opened and two young kids came out. 'Come in, Marcus,' said Mrs Morrison.

Marcus's talk with Mrs Morrison didn't go very well. She asked him about the boys who stole his trainers and he said he didn't know who they were. This wasn't true, of course, but he didn't want any more trouble from them.

'Marcus, if the other kids are bullying you, why don't you just keep out of their way?'

Marcus was annoyed. Did she think he was stupid? Did she think he went looking for trouble? 'I have tried,' he said.

'Maybe you haven't tried hard enough.'

Marcus stood up to go. He'd had enough. She wasn't going to be helpful because she didn't like him. Nobody at this school liked him and he didn't understand why.

'Sit down, Marcus. I haven't finished with you.'

'But I've finished with you.'

He had never been rude to a teacher before and he was very surprised at himself. He walked out of Mrs Morrison's office, and out of the school.

Marcus was walking slowly along Upper Street when Will saw him. Will was driving back from the supermarket, listening to loud music in his car. What was Marcus doing out of school at two o'clock in the afternoon? he wondered.

At exactly 4.15 that afternoon, right in the middle of *Countdown*, Marcus rang his doorbell. At first Will didn't answer, but Marcus rang and rang. Will turned off the TV and put on some music by the pop group Nirvana, hoping that Marcus would go away. But Marcus didn't stop ringing the bell, so finally Will opened the door and let him in.

'You shouldn't be here.'

'I came to ask you something. I want you to take me and a friend to a football match.'

'You don't like football.'

'I do now,' said Marcus. 'I like Manchester United. And I like a player called Kirk O'Bane. He's got long blond hair and a beard.'

'Marcus, there isn't a player called O'Bane who plays for Manchester United. I know all the players and there's nobody with long blond hair and a beard. There was a player called O'Kane who played for Nottingham about twenty-five years ago. What lessons did you have this afternoon?'

Marcus looked at him, trying to work out why he was asking the question. 'History, and then ... umm ...'

'Marcus, I saw you this afternoon.'

'What, in school?'

'Well, I didn't see you in school, did I? Because you weren't there. I drove past you on Upper Street.'

'It was Mrs Morrison's fault. The head teacher. She told me to keep out of their way – the boys who stole my trainers.' Marcus began to get upset, and to speak more quickly. 'They followed me! How can I keep out of their way if they follow me?'

'All right, Marcus, calm down. Did you tell her that?'

'Of course. But she didn't take any notice.'

'Right. So go home and tell your mum this. It's no good telling me.'

'I'm not telling her. She's got enough problems without me. Why can't you go and see her? Mrs Morrison.'

'You're joking. Listen, Marcus. I'm not your father, or your uncle, or any member of your family. No head teacher is going to take any notice of what I say. You've got to stop thinking I know the answer to anything, because I don't.'

'You know about things. You knew about the trainers. And you know about Kirk O'Bane. The footballer.'

Suddenly Will realized who Marcus was talking about. 'It's not Kirk O'Bane, you fool, it's Kurt Cobain. The singer with Nirvana.'

'I thought he must be a singer,' said Marcus. 'I didn't know about him, and my mum wouldn't either, but you did. You see, you know things. You can help.'

It was then, for the first time, that Will understood the kind of help that Marcus needed. Fiona had given him the idea that Marcus needed an adult male in his life, but that was wrong. Marcus needed help to be a kid. And, unfortunately for Will, that was exactly the kind of help that he could give. Will couldn't tell Marcus how to grow up, or how to **cope** with a mother who wanted to kill herself. But he could certainly tell him that Kurt Cobain wasn't a footballer.

Marcus went back to school the following day. Nobody had noticed that he had been absent the afternoon before, so he didn't get into trouble. In the morning break he found Ellie and a friend from her class, Zoe, by the drinks machine. Ellie was wearing her Kurt Cobain sweatshirt.

'Kurt Cobain doesn't play for Manchester United,' he told her. 'He plays ... he *sings* ... for Nirvana. A friend of mine has got one of their CDs. *Nevermind.*'

'Thanks for telling me,' said Ellie and laughed. 'What year's your friend in? I didn't think anyone in this school liked Nirvana. And what do you think of them?'

'He's left school. He's quite old. And I don't know what I think of Nirvana.' Will had played him some of their music the evening before. It had been very

cope /kəʊp/ (v) to manage a situation successfully

noisy with a lot of shouting, but there had been some quiet bits too. He didn't think he would ever like it as much as Joni Mitchell or Mozart, but he could understand why Ellie might like it.

'It's a bit noisy,' said Marcus, 'but the picture on the cover is very interesting.' It was a picture of a baby, swimming after a dollar note. Will had said something about the picture, but he couldn't remember what it was. 'I think the cover has a meaning. Something about society.'

Ellie and Zoe looked at each other and laughed.

'You're very funny,' said Zoe. 'Who are you?'

'Marcus.'

'Cool name,' said Zoe, and they laughed again. 'See you around, Marcus.'

It was the longest conversation he'd had with anyone at school for weeks.

Later, he told Will about Ellie.

'Can I invite her round to your flat?' he asked.

'I'm not sure she'd come, Marcus. How old is she? Fifteen? I'm not sure fifteen-year-old girls want to go around with twelve-year-old boys. She probably has a 25-year-old boyfriend who rides a Harley Davidson.'

Marcus hadn't thought of that. 'I don't want to go out with her. She wouldn't be interested in someone like me. But we can come round here and listen to your Nirvana CDs, can't we?'

'She's probably heard them already.'

Marcus was getting annoyed with Will. Why didn't he want him to make friends? 'OK, forget it, then.'

'I'm sorry, Marcus. I'm glad you spoke to Ellie today. But a two-minute conversation with someone who's laughing at you ... I'm not sure this relationship is going to last.'

Marcus wasn't listening. Ellie and her friend had said he was funny, and he'd made them laugh. That had made him feel good, and he knew he could make them laugh again. The next day he saw them again by the drinks machine.

'Ellie, how old is your boyfriend?' The girls laughed and Marcus felt happy. 'My friend Will said he's probably about twenty-five and rides a Harley Davidson.'

'He's a hundred and two,' said Ellie. 'How old's your girlfriend? She probably wants to kill me, doesn't she?'

'I haven't got one,' said Marcus, and the girls laughed again. They were laughing all the time now.

Ellie and Zoe came looking for Marcus at lunchtime. He was at his desk eating sandwiches when they came into his classroom, calling his name. Almost every kid in the room stopped what they were doing and turned round. You could see what they were thinking: Ellie and *Marcus*? Even Nicky and Mark, who hadn't spoken to him for weeks, looked up from their Gameboy.

'What are you all staring at? Marcus is our friend, aren't you, Marcus? Let's go to our classroom. You don't want to stay here with these boring little kids, do you?'

Some of the kids turned red, but nobody said anything. Nobody wanted to argue with Ellie. They watched as Marcus walked from his desk to where Ellie and Zoe were standing. When he got there, Ellie gave him a kiss.

Marcus felt very proud as he walked through the school with Ellie and Zoe. The other kids, and even the teachers, stared at them in surprise. When they got to Ellie's classroom, Ellie made him stand outside. He could hear her shouting to the other kids.

'OK, listen, everybody. I want you to meet Marcus. He's the only other person in the whole school who likes Kurt Cobain. Come in, Marcus.'

He walked in, and everybody laughed when they saw him. Ellie and Zoe stood beside him and Marcus felt great.

4.1 Were you right?

Look back at your answers to Activity 3.4. Then choose the correct endings to these sentences. Circle a or b.

1 Marcus goes to Will's flat because ...
  a he is invited.
  b he doesn't want to go home.

2 Ellie likes Marcus because ...
  a he is different from the other kids.
  b he is a good singer.

4.2 What more did you learn?

1 Put the sentences in the correct order.

Chapter 5

a ☐ Will buys Marcus some new trainers.
b ☐ Fiona is angry with Will.
c ☐1 Some kids throw sweets at Marcus.
d ☐ Marcus's trainers are stolen.

Chapter 6

e ☐ Marcus walks angrily out of school.
f ☐ Ellie decides that Marcus is OK.
g ☐ Marcus goes to see the head teacher.
h ☐ Will explains about the singer Kurt Cobain.

2 **Will watches *Countdown*, 'the most boring programme in the history of television'. Play this game, which is similar to one on the programme.**

  a Choose three letters from Box A and write them in the first three spaces at the bottom of the page.

  b Choose six letters from Box B and write them in the last six spaces.

  c Change books with another student. You have three minutes. Who can make the longest English word from the letters in front of them? The letters can be in any order. Write your longest word in Box C.

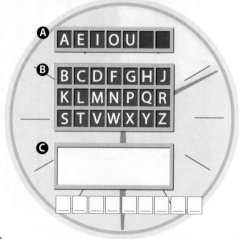

4.3 **Language in use**

Look at the sentences in the box.
Then complete the reported
statements below.

> He **said** he **didn't know** who they were.
>
> I **told** you I **didn't want** to see Marcus again.

I hate going to the hairdresser.

Will bought me some trainers.

Marcus is doing fine.

If you need new clothes, I'll get them.

Will's not going to open the door.

I can tell you about music.

1 Marcus said (that) ...he hated going to the hairdresser... .

2 Marcus told his mum (that) ....

3 Fiona told Will (that) ....

4 Fiona told Marcus (that) ....

5 Fiona said (that) ....

6 Will told Marcus (that) ....

4.4 **What happens next?**

1 Look at the title of Chapter 7, and the words in *italics* below it. Complete the
   sentences with your ideas.

   1 .... spends Christmas with Fiona and Marcus.

   2 .... defends Will from ....

2 Look at the title of Chapter 8, and the words in *italics* below it. Complete the
   sentences with your ideas.

   1 .... falls in love with a girl at a party.

   2 Will asks Marcus to pretend to be his son because ....

   ....

CHAPTER 7

Christmas at Fiona's

'Why is everyone being so horrible to him?
He only pretended to have a kid for a couple of weeks. That's nothing.'

Will was feeling depressed. It was only 19 November, but he had heard his dad's Christmas song in a supermarket that morning.

Will hated Christmas: people knocked on his door, singing the song he hated more than any other song in the world, and expected him to give them money. His dad had hated Christmas too, but for a different reason: it reminded him of how badly he had failed in his life. His famous Christmas song was the only successful song he had ever written. At Christmas, Will's dad had always got depressed and angry and drunk a lot, so it had never been a very happy time for Will.

Since his parents had died, Will had usually spent the holiday with friends, or girlfriends' families, but this year he had no plans. There was no girlfriend, and so there were no girlfriend's parents. He decided that he would sit at home and watch old films on TV and get drunk, but that didn't seem very Christmassy.

He thought about spending Christmas Day with a family – not his family, because he didn't have one, but *a* family. He definitely didn't want to spend Christmas with Marcus and Fiona, though – eating vegetarian food, not watching TV, singing Christmas songs with his eyes closed. But the next afternoon Marcus came round and invited Will to spend Christmas with them.

'Ummm,' said Will. 'That's ... very kind of you.'

'But you're coming?'

'I don't know.'

'Why not?'

'Because ...'

'Don't you want to come?'

'Yes, of course I do, but ... what about your mum?'

'She'll be there too.'

'Yes, I know. But she wouldn't want me there.'

'I've already spoken to her about it. I said I wanted to invite a friend, and she said OK. She guessed it was you. I haven't got any other friends.'

'All right,' Will said at last. 'I'd love to spend Christmas with you, Marcus.'

When he arrived at Marcus and Fiona's flat on Christmas Day, he was pleased to find other people there too. There was Marcus's dad Clive, and his girlfriend Lindsey, and his girlfriend's mum, all sitting in a line on the sofa. Will was very surprised that Fiona and Clive were still friendly although their relationship had

finished some time ago. The people in SPAT hadn't been like that about their broken relationships – they had been angry and unhappy.

Will gave Marcus a CD of *Nevermind* and a Kurt Cobain T-shirt, and Marcus gave Will a book of *Countdown* quizzes. Fiona gave Will *The Single Parent's Guide* as a joke.

'What's the joke?' asked Lindsey.

'Nothing,' said Will quickly.

'Will pretended to have a kid so he could join a single parents' group,' Marcus told her.

'Oh,' Lindsey said. She and her mum and Clive looked at Will with interest, but he just smiled.

Clive gave Marcus some computer games and CDs and sweatshirts. But Fiona's presents to Marcus weren't very interesting at all, Will thought – books, and a hairy jumper, and some piano music. But Marcus was really pleased with them, and for the first time Will understood that Marcus was a good kid. He didn't need expensive presents to be happy.

They had lunch and then watched TV. Marcus was happy and Will felt very relaxed. But later in the afternoon Suzie arrived with Megan. Fiona had told her that Will didn't really have a two-year-old son called Ned, but Will hadn't seen Suzie since then and now he felt really embarrassed and ashamed. He stood up, and then he sat down again, and then he stood up again and said he had to go.

'Don't be so silly, Will,' said Fiona.

So Will sat down again and Suzie sat next to him, but she refused to speak to him.

Megan went over to the Christmas tree and Fiona handed her a present. 'This is for you, Megan,' she said.

Megan stood holding her present and looked around the room. Then she walked over to Will and tried to give it to him. Will didn't move.

'Well, take it from her, you fool,' said Suzie.

'It's not my present,' said Will, but Megan continued to hold it out until he reached for it. 'Now what?' he said.

'Open it with her,' said Suzie.

Will helped Megan open the present. It was a plastic musical toy. They both looked at it.

'Now play with her,' Suzie said angrily. 'It's easy to see that you don't know anything about kids. But you should learn. It would be useful to you in your kind of work.'

'What is your kind of work?' asked Lindsey politely.

'He doesn't do anything,' Marcus said. 'His dad wrote a famous song and he earns a million pounds a minute.'

'He pretends he has a child so he can join single parents' groups and meet single mothers,' said Suzie.

'Yes, but he doesn't get paid for that,' said Marcus.

Will stood up again, but this time he didn't sit down. 'Thanks for the lunch,' he said. 'I'm going home now.'

'Suzie has a right to be angry with you,' Fiona said.

'Yes, and now I have a right to go home.'

'But I don't want him to go yet,' said Marcus suddenly. 'He's my friend. I invited him. I should be able to tell him when he goes home. Why is everyone being so horrible to him? He only pretended to have a kid for a couple of weeks. That's nothing. Kids at school do worse than that every day.'

'Yes, but Will isn't a kid,' said Suzie.

'Yes, but he's behaved better since then. He never wanted me round his flat every day. I just went. And he bought me those shoes and he listens when I say I'm having a bad time at school. And he knew who Kirk O'Bane was.'

'Kurt Cobain,' said Will.

'And you all do wrong things too sometimes,' said Marcus. 'I mean ...' He had to be careful here. He knew he couldn't say anything about the hospital or Fiona. 'I mean, how did I first become friends with Will?'

'You threw a great big loaf of bread at a duck's head and killed it,' said Will.

Suzie and Fiona started laughing.

'Is that true, Marcus?' asked his father.

'There was something wrong with it,' Marcus said. 'I think it was going to die anyway.'

Suzie and Fiona laughed even more. The three people on the sofa looked shocked. Will sat down again.

CHAPTER 8

Falling in Love

'I want you to pretend to be my son,' he said.
'But why?' asked Marcus. 'I don't understand.'

W ill met a woman called Rachel at a party on New Year's Eve,* and fell in love
with her. He'd never wanted to fall in love because he'd always thought of
it as a very unpleasant experience. He had watched it happen to friends, and had
seen them lose weight and sleep and become unhappy. He was sure that Rachel
was going to make him very unhappy, because he didn't think she would find him
interesting.

Rachel was beautiful and intelligent and she did drawings for children's books.
She sat down next to Will at dinner and asked him questions, but he couldn't

* New Year's Eve: 31 December; the day before New Year's Day

think of anything to say. Most people at the party worked in television, or had other interesting jobs, but Will didn't have a job and he hadn't done anything interesting with his life. He watched *Countdown* and drove around listening to Nirvana.

The most interesting thing about his life, Will suddenly realized, was Marcus. He could see that Rachel was quickly losing interest in him. She had begun to talk to the person sitting on her other side and they were having a conversation about pop music. Rachel was saying that to her Nirvana sounded just like the sixties group Led Zeppelin.

'I know a twelve-year-old boy who would kill you for saying that,' said Will. It wasn't true, of course. Marcus had only just started listening to Nirvana, and he didn't know anything about Led Zeppelin. But Rachel was interested.

'So do I,' she said. 'Maybe they should meet. What's yours called?'

He's not mine, exactly, Will thought. 'Marcus.'

'Mine's Ali.'

'Right.'

'And is Marcus's mother here tonight?'

'Ummm ...' Will looked up and down the table. 'No.' It wasn't a lie! Fiona wasn't there.

'You're not spending New Year's Eve with her?'

'No. We ... er ... don't live together.' This wasn't a lie either. He didn't live with Fiona, he had never lived with Fiona and he never intended to live with her in the future. 'How about Ali's dad?'

'He lives in America.'

'Right.'

Rachel started to talk about Ali's father and Will listened. He was very good at listening when a woman told him how badly her ex-husband had behaved. He had heard the same story many times from the women in SPAT.

At midnight Will and Rachel kissed, and at half-past twelve, just before Rachel left, they arranged for Marcus and Ali to meet and compare computer games and CDs.

Now Will had a problem. He had allowed Rachel to believe that he had a twelve-year-old son because it made him more interesting. He was going to have to talk to Marcus, and he knew the conversation would be difficult. So he took Marcus out to a place full of video machines.

'I want you to pretend to be my son,' he said.

'But why?' asked Marcus. 'I don't understand.'

'Because I've met a woman who thinks you're my son.'

'Why don't you tell her I'm not your son?'

'No.'

'Why not? I'll tell her if you like. I don't mind.'

'That's very kind of you, Marcus, but it wouldn't help.'

Marcus was busy playing one of the video games. 'Why not? I don't understand.'

'Marcus, listen. I'm really interested in this woman. I let her believe you were my son because that's the only reason she might be interested in me.'

'What do you mean, you're really interested in her? Why is she so interesting?'

'I **fancy** this woman, Marcus. I want to go out with her. I want her to be my girlfriend.'

At last Marcus turned away from the video machine and looked at Will, his eyes shining. 'Really?'

'Yes, really.' Will wanted Rachel to be his wife, his lover, the centre of his world.

'How do you know you want her to be your girlfriend?'

'I don't know. I just feel it.'

'Oh,' said Marcus. 'Well, I feel the same about Ellie. I want her to be my girlfriend.'

'You want Ellie to be your girlfriend? Not just a friend?'

'Well,' said Marcus, 'I want to be with her all the time. And I want to tell her things before I tell anyone, even you or mum. And I don't want her to have another boyfriend.'

So Marcus agreed to help Will. Will called Rachel and Rachel invited them to lunch the following Saturday. Marcus came round to Will's flat just after midday. He was wearing the hairy **jumper** that he got from Fiona for Christmas and a pair of bright yellow trousers. Will looked cool: he was wearing his favourite shirt and a black leather jacket.

'Listen,' said Marcus in the car on the way over to Rachel's place. 'If you're my dad, you should know some things about me. When's my birthday?'

'I don't know.'

'August the nineteenth. And what's my favourite food?'

'Tell me.'

'Pizza. And where did I go on my first trip abroad?'

'France.'

'No, Spain. And who's my mum?'

'What?' The question was such an important one that Will couldn't think what to say. 'Your mum's your mum.'

---

fancy /ˈfænsi/ (v) to feel sexually attracted to someone

jumper /ˈdʒʌmpə/ (n) a piece of woollen clothing that covers the upper part of your body and your arms

'So you were married to my mum and then you separated. Are you worried about that? Am I?'

The questions seemed so silly that both Marcus and Will began to laugh. They laughed and laughed, and couldn't stop.

Rachel lived in a tall, thin house full of books and old furniture and photographs. It had a warm, welcoming feel, very different from Will's cool modern flat.

'Come in, both of you,' Rachel said. 'Come and meet Ali.' She shouted up the stairs: 'Ali!' No reply. 'ALI!' Still no reply. She looked at Will. 'He's got his **headphones** on. Shall we go up?'

They went upstairs. Ali's bedroom was typical of a twelve-year-old boy, with large pictures of singers and sexy actresses on the wall. Ali was bent over his computer with his headphones on, and didn't hear them come in. His mother touched him on the shoulder and he jumped.

'Oh, hi. Sorry.' Ali stood up and Will immediately saw that Ali and Marcus were very different. Ali was cool, with fashionable boots and trousers, long hair and even an earring. His face seemed to darken when he saw Marcus's yellow trousers and hairy jumper.

'Marcus – Ali, Ali – Marcus,' said Rachel. 'Do you guys want to stay up here?'

Marcus looked at Will. 'Yes,' he said, and for a moment Will loved him.

'OK,' said Ali, but he didn't sound very enthusiastic.

Marcus knew the lunch with Rachel was very important to Will, and he wanted to help as much as possible. He also thought that if he helped Will with Rachel, then Will might help him with Ellie. But Ali never gave him a chance.

'It isn't going to happen,' he said when Rachel and Will had gone downstairs.

'No?' said Marcus, although he didn't know what Ali was talking about.

'If your dad goes out with my mum, you're dead.'

'Oh, he's all right,' said Marcus.

Ali stared at him. 'I don't care if he's all right. I don't want him going out with my mum. So I don't want to see you or him round here ever again, OK?'

'Can I use the computer? What games have you got?' Marcus said, trying to change the subject.

'Are you listening to me?'

'Yes, but … I'm not sure there's very much I can do at the moment. We've come for lunch, and Will … that's my dad, but I call him Will … he's talking to your mum downstairs and he's really **keen on** her, and who knows? She might be keen on him, so …'

headphones /ˈhedfəʊnz/ (n pl) equipment that you wear over your ears to listen to a recording
be keen on /bi ˈkiːn ɒn/ to like someone or something very much

61

'SHE'S NOT KEEN ON HIM!' Ali suddenly shouted. 'SHE'S ONLY KEEN ON ME!'

Marcus was beginning to realize that Ali was crazy, and he wasn't sure what to do about it. He thought it would be dangerous to stay in Ali's room. He could go downstairs and join Will and Rachel, but he would have to explain that Ali was crazy, and that would be really embarrassing. He decided to run downstairs and out of the front door, and get a bus home.

He was standing at a bus stop when Will drove up beside him and told him to get into the car.

'What are you doing?' asked Will angrily. 'What happened upstairs?'

'Ali's crazy. He said he'd kill me if you went out with Rachel. And I believed him. He's really frightening. Where are we going now?'

It was raining now and the streets were full of traffic and people out shopping. Everywhere Marcus looked, there were people with long, wet hair.

'Back to Rachel's.'

'I don't want to go back there. She'll think I'm stupid.'

'She won't. She thought something like this might happen. She said Ali could be difficult sometimes. Anyway, he's crying like a three-year-old child.'

'Really?' Suddenly Marcus felt better. He was quite happy to go back to Rachel's, he decided.

'Ali has got something to say to you, Marcus,' said Rachel when they walked in.

'Sorry, Marcus,' said Ali. 'I didn't mean to say those things.'

Marcus wasn't sure if he believed Ali. How could you say that you were going to kill someone by mistake? But Ali was crying, and that made Marcus feel generous.

'That's OK, Ali,' he said.

Rachel made Ali and Marcus shake hands.

'Ali finds this kind of thing very difficult,' she said.

Will smiled. 'It's OK,' he said gently, and Rachel looked at him and smiled back. Suddenly Marcus could see why nice, attractive women like Rachel and Suzie might like Will. He had a way of looking at them that he had never used on Marcus – there was something in his eyes, a kind of softness. Would Ellie like him if he did that? She'd probably hit him.

'My last boyfriend was ... anyway, he and Ali didn't like each other. I'm sorry, I'm not comparing you to him. I have no idea whether ... I mean, I don't know, I just thought on New Year's Eve ... oh, this is so embarrassing. It's all your fault, Ali. We shouldn't have to talk about this now.'

'It's OK,' said Marcus brightly. 'Will really fancies you. He told me.'

5.1 Were you right?

Look back at your answers to Activity 4.4. Discuss these questions and then write your answers.

1 How many people spend Christmas at Fiona's flat? Who are they?

....

2 Who is angry with Will? Why?

....

3 Who does Will fall in love with? What is she like?

....

4 What is her son's name? What is he like?

....

5.2 What more did you learn?

Whose thoughts might these be? Match them with the pictures.

(1) 'I don't hate Clive.'

A

(2) 'He must let me have a boyfriend.'

B

(3) 'I think I'm in love with Rachel.'

C

(4) 'I want to help him with Rachel.'

D

(5) 'He knows nothing about children.'

E

(6) 'I don't want my mum to have a boyfriend.'

F

(7) 'He's nice. I like him a lot.'

5.3 Language in use

Look at the sentences in the box. Then make sentences below with *should* or *shouldn't*.

> You **should know** some things about me.
>
> We **shouldn't have to** talk about this now.

1 Will / alone at Christmas
   Will shouldn't be alone at Christmas.

2 Marcus / more friends.

3 Fiona / more relaxed.

4 Ali / about his mother's boyfriends.

5 Families / so complicated!

5.4 What happens next?

1 **Look at the title of Chapter 9, and the words in *italics* below it. Then discuss this question and make notes. What do you think?**

Notes
How will love change Will?

2 **Look at the title of Chapter 10, and the words in *italics* below it. Discuss the questions and make notes. What do you think?**

Notes
Who goes to Cambridge? Why is Marcus in a police station?

CHAPTER 9

Depressions

*Will was in love with Rachel and everything had changed.
For the first time in his life he wanted to be deeply involved with someone.*

Will wanted to spend the rest of his life with Rachel, and he knew that he couldn't continue pretending to her that Marcus was his son. So he told her the truth one evening when they were having dinner in a Chinese restaurant.

'Oh,' said Rachel. 'So who's his natural father?'

'It's a guy called Clive who lives in Cambridge.'

'Right. And are you friendly with him?'

'Yes. We spent Christmas together, actually.'

'So ... if you're not Marcus's natural father, and you don't live with him ... how is he your son?'

'Yes,' said Will. 'It must look very confusing from the outside.'

'Tell me how it is on the inside.'

'It's just that kind of relationship. I'm old enough to be his father, he's old enough to be my son ...'

'Did you ever live with Marcus's mother?'

'No. Listen, I never actually said he was my son. The words "I have a son called Marcus" never passed my lips. That's what you chose to believe.'

'You mean ... I wanted to believe you had a son, so I just imagined it? I'm the one who was imagining things?' Clearly Rachel thought that Will was crazy. But he felt she was beginning to see the funny side of the situation too. 'But what about Marcus? You didn't just hire him for the afternoon. There's some kind of relationship there.'

So Will told her everything about Marcus. Nearly everything, anyway; he didn't tell her that he'd first met Marcus because he'd joined SPAT. He didn't think she would understand about SPAT. She might think he had some kind of problem.

Rachel invited him back to her flat after the meal and they sat drinking coffee out of big blue cups.

'Why did you think Marcus would make you more interesting?' she asked.

'Was I more interesting?'

'Yes, I suppose you were.'

'Why?'

'Because ... you really want to know the truth? Because you seemed to be a shallow kind of person. You didn't do anything; you didn't seem to care about anything or have much to say – and then when you said you had a kid ...'

'I didn't actually say ...'

'I realized that I'd made a mistake about you. And I *had* made a mistake. You do care about Marcus, and you understand him, and you worry about him. You're not the shallow kind of guy I thought you were.'

Will knew that Rachel was trying to make him feel better about everything, but he still felt bad. He'd known Marcus for only a few months, so what about the thirty-six years before that? And he didn't want to be interesting only because of his relationship with Marcus. He wanted to be interesting for himself.

Will was in love with Rachel and everything had changed. For the first time in his life he wanted to be deeply involved with someone.

◆

Three or four weeks passed. Marcus saw Will, and he saw Ellie and Zoe at school. Will bought him some new glasses, and took him to have his hair cut, and played him some music by singers who he liked and Ellie didn't hate. He felt that he was changing, in his own body and in his head, and then his mum started crying again.

Just like before, there didn't seem to be any reason for it. Finally, she started crying at breakfast again and Marcus knew that things were serious and that they were in trouble.

But one thing had changed for Marcus. When she had started crying at breakfast before, he had been alone. Now he had Will and Ellie.

'My mum's started crying again,' he said to Will. It was a Thursday afternoon and they were in Will's kitchen, making toast.

'Oh,' said Will. 'Are you worried about it?'

'Of course. She's the same now as she was before. Worse.' That wasn't true. Nothing could be worse than the last time, but he wanted to make sure Will knew it was serious.

'So what are you going to do?'

Marcus had thought that Will would help him. That's what he wanted. Wasn't that what friends were for?

'What am *I* going to do? What are *you* going to do?'

'What am *I* going to do?' Will laughed, and then remembered that the situation wasn't funny. 'Marcus, I can't do anything.'

'You could talk to her.'

'Why should she listen to me? Who am I? Nobody.'

'You're not nobody. You're ...'

'You come round here for a cup of tea after school, but that doesn't mean I can make your mum feel better. I know I can't.'

'I thought we were friends.'

'Yes, Marcus, we're friends. But I'm not your dad, I'm not your uncle, and I'm not your big brother. I can tell you who Kurt Cobain is and what trainers to get, and that's all. Do you understand?'

'Yes.'

But on the way home, Marcus thought about the way Will had said, 'Do you understand?' to end the conversation. He knew teachers said that, and parents said that, but he didn't think friends said that.

He wasn't really surprised about Will. He thought of Ellie as his best friend more than Will – not just because he loved her and wanted to go out with her, but because she was always nice to him. Ellie had told him that she knew about his mum trying to kill herself. Ellie's mum was a friend of Suzie's, and Suzie had told her.

But the next day, when Marcus went to find Ellie in her classroom at breaktime, she didn't seem very pleased to see him. Zoe was sitting next to her, holding her hand.

'What's happened?' he asked.

'Haven't you heard?'

Marcus hated it when people said that to him because he never had. 'I don't think so.'

'Kurt Cobain.'

'What about him?'

'He tried to kill himself. He took a lot of pills.'

'Is he all right?'

'I think so. They pumped his stomach.'

'Good.'

'Nothing's good,' said Ellie. 'He'll do it, you know, in the end. They always do. He wants to die. It wasn't a cry for help. He hates this world.'

Marcus suddenly felt sick. He'd imagined having a conversation with Ellie about his mum, and Ellie making him feel better, but it wasn't like that at all.

'How do you know?'

'You don't know him,' said Ellie.

'*You* don't know him,' Marcus shouted. 'He's not even a real person. He's just a singer. He's just someone on a sweatshirt. It's not like he's anyone's mum.'

'No, but he's someone's dad,' said Ellie. 'He's got a beautiful little girl and he still wants to die.'

Marcus was very upset. He turned round and ran out. Did his mum feel the same way as Kurt Cobain? He went to the boys' toilets and shut himself inside the end toilet because it had hot water pipes running along the wall and you could sit on them. After a few minutes someone came in and started kicking on the door.

'Are you in there, Marcus?' said Ellie. 'I'm sorry. I'd forgotten about your mum. It's OK. She's not like Kurt. She's not going to try to kill herself again.'

He paused for a moment, then unlocked the door and looked out. 'How do you know?'

'Because you're right about him. He's not a real person.'

'You're only saying that to make me feel better.'

'OK, he's a real person. But he's a different kind of real person. He's like James Dean and Marilyn Monroe and Jimi Hendrix and all those people. He's not like your mum. You think I know things, but I don't. I don't know why Kurt Cobain feels like he does, or why your mum feels like she does. And I don't know what it feels like to be you. Quite frightening, I should think.'

'Yes.' Marcus started to cry then. It wasn't noisy crying – his eyes just filled with tears and they ran down his face – but it was still embarrassing. He'd never thought he'd cry in front of Ellie.

She came in and put her arm round him. 'Don't listen to me. You know more than I do. You should be telling me things.'

They sat on the hot water pipes together in silence, moving when they got too hot, and waited until they felt like going back into the world.

◆

Will knew that he should do something about Fiona and that he'd behaved badly towards Marcus. He was older than Marcus, he knew more ... He should get involved, help the kid, look after him.

But he didn't want to have a conversation with Fiona about her depression. She would ask him what the meaning of life was – ask him why she should go on living. And Will couldn't tell her what the meaning was, because he didn't know. But Fiona was lost and unhappy, and if he told her that life had no meaning, she might actually kill herself.

He decided to talk to Rachel about Fiona. They were in Rachel's kitchen, making coffee.

'A few years ago I got very depressed,' said Rachel, 'and I thought about killing myself, like Fiona. But I always thought I would do it tomorrow, never today. There were always a lot of reasons to continue living; there were too many things that I'd started but hadn't finished, and I wanted to see what happened.'

'Fiona must have things like that too.'

'I don't know,' said Rachel. 'Perhaps she doesn't. Why don't *I* talk to her?'

'You? She doesn't know you.'

'It doesn't matter. And maybe you could learn to help her too, if I showed you how. It's not so bad.'

'OK,' said Will, but he didn't want to think about Fiona just at that moment. He couldn't remember ever feeling as happy as he did with Rachel.

CHAPTER 10

A Trip to Cambridge

There was a message from Marcus, but he didn't sound OK.
He was calling from a police station ... and he sounded frightened and lonely.

It was spring and the days were getting longer. Now Marcus was able to walk home from Will's flat in the late afternoon sunshine. He began to feel better about things. Then his dad fell down some steps and broke his arm.

'You'll have to go up to Cambridge and see him,' said his mum.

'I'm not going while you're like this.'

'Like what?'

'Crying all the time.'

'I'm OK. Well, I'm not OK, but I'm not going to do anything silly. I promise.'

'But why do I have to go and see him?'

'He was asking for you. He's lucky he didn't hurt himself really badly. Maybe he's having a big think about his life.'

That made Marcus angry. He went and sat in his room. Why had his dad never had a big think about his life before? And why did he only want to see his son when he'd broken his arm? What about all the hundreds of days when his arm was all right, and Marcus had heard nothing from him?

He went downstairs again. 'I'm not going,' he told his mum. 'He makes me sick.'

But the next day, when he told Ellie about his dad, he began to change his mind.

'You should go and see him,' said Ellie. 'Tell him what you think of him. I'll come with you, if you like.'

Marcus thought how nice it would be to have a whole hour with Ellie on the train to Cambridge.

'Will you come with me really, Ellie?'

'Yes, of course. If you want me to. It would be fun. I'll know what to say to him.'

Marcus didn't stop to think about what Ellie was going to say to his father. He'd worry about that later.

'So shall we go next week, then?' It was nearly Easter, and they were on holiday from school next week, so they could stay in Cambridge for the night if they wanted to.

'Yes. Cool. We'll have a great time.'

Marcus and Ellie arranged to meet at King's Cross station in north London, where they would catch the train to Cambridge. Fiona wanted to come to the station with him, but he didn't want her to see Ellie.

'It would be too sad,' he told her. 'I don't want to say goodbye to you there.'

So Fiona and Marcus walked from their flat to Holloway Road underground station and said goodbye in the entrance. Fiona gave Marcus an enormous **hug**, while everyone around them watched.

The underground train wasn't crowded. It was the middle of the afternoon and there was only one other person in the same part of the train, an old guy reading a newspaper. He was looking at the back page, so Marcus could see the front.

The photo seemed so familiar that for a moment he thought it was a picture of someone he knew, like a member of the family. But none of his relatives had long blond hair and half a beard.

He knew who it was now. He saw the same picture every day of the week on Ellie's sweatshirt. He felt hot all over; he didn't even need to read the old guy's paper, but he did.

ROCK STAR COBAIN DEAD, it said in big letters, and then underneath, in smaller writing, *Nirvana singer, 27, shoots himself.* Marcus thought and felt a lot of things at the same time. He wondered whether Ellie had seen the paper yet, and how she would be when she found out. He wondered if his mum was OK, although he knew there was no connection between his mum and Kurt Cobain because his mum was a real person and Kurt Cobain wasn't.

Then he felt confused because the newspaper had turned Kurt Cobain into a real person. And then he felt very sad – sad for Ellie, sad for Kurt Cobain's wife and little girl, sad for his mum, sad for himself. And then he was at King's Cross and he had to get off the train. He met Ellie under the information board. She seemed normal.

Everyone was carrying a newspaper, so Kurt Cobain was everywhere. There was a whole army of Kurt Cobains marching towards them. Marcus didn't know what to do. He didn't want Ellie to learn that Kurt Cobain was dead. Then he had an idea.

'Ellie,' he said suddenly. 'Do you trust me? Yes or no?'

'What are you talking about? Of course I trust you.'

'OK, then. Close your eyes and hang on to my jacket.'

'What? Why?'

'I watched a programme on TV with my mum once. It was all about learning to trust someone. They made some people close their eyes and then other people led them around and made sure that they didn't hurt themselves.'

hug /hʌg/ (n/v) the act of putting your arms around someone in a loving way and holding them tightly

'Marcus, have you gone mad?'

'I'm going to guide you to the train through all these people, and then you'll trust me for ever.'

'Oh, all right.'

Ellie closed her eyes and Marcus led her to the part of the station where the Cambridge train was waiting. She didn't see all the people with newspapers coming towards them. Marcus was almost enjoying it, because he liked the feeling of looking after Ellie.

'Are we nearly there?'

'Yes. The train's there waiting for us.'

'I know why you're doing this, Marcus,' she said suddenly in a small, quiet voice. He stopped, but she continued to hold him. 'You think I haven't seen the paper, but I have.'

He turned round, but she didn't open her eyes.

'Are you OK?'

'Yes. Well, not really.' She felt around in her bag and got out a bottle of **vodka**. 'I'm going to get drunk.'

◆

Will had arranged to go to a pub in Islington with Rachel and Fiona while Marcus was in Cambridge visiting his father. They would all have a drink and a talk, then Will would leave and Rachel and Fiona would have another drink and a talk. Fiona would feel better about things, and not want to kill herself. What could possibly go wrong?

Will arrived at the pub first, got himself a drink, sat down and lit a cigarette, and Fiona arrived soon afterwards. But Rachel didn't come. Half an hour passed and she still hadn't arrived. Will went to phone her, but he only got through to her answer machine. Then he realized the truth. She had never intended to come because she wanted Will to talk to Fiona by himself. She had said he could learn to help Fiona if she showed him how, and this was what she meant.

Will didn't know what to do. He went back to his seat and he and Fiona sat in silence for some time. Then Fiona started to cry. At first Will tried not to take any notice of her, but he couldn't. He knew he would have to try and help.

'What's the matter?' he asked.

'Nothing.'

'That's not true, is it?'

'Yes, it is. Nothing's the matter – no thing. I'm just like this. I think I probably need to talk to somebody.'

'Do you want to go and get something to eat?' said Will.

vodka /ˈvɒdkə/ (n) a strong, clear alcoholic drink

They went to a pizza restaurant on Upper Street.

'I'm sorry for being like this,' said Fiona. 'And for being like this with you.'

Will started to make a joke, but then he thought he would try to say something serious and useful.

'I'm the one who should apologize,' he said. 'I want to help, but I know I won't be able to. I haven't got the answers to anything.'

'I don't need answers,' said Fiona. 'I know there's nothing you can do. I'm depressed. It's an illness. It just started. Well, that's not true ... there were some things that happened ...'

Suddenly Fiona started talking about her problems. It was much easier than Will had thought; he just had to listen, and ask the right questions. He'd done it before, lots of times, with Angie and Suzie and Rachel, but that was for a reason. This was different. He didn't want to sleep with Fiona, but he did want to make her feel better.

He learnt a lot of things about her. He learnt that she hadn't really wanted to be a mother and that sometimes she hated Marcus; he learnt that she was worried about not having a relationship and that her last birthday had depressed her

because she hadn't been anywhere or done anything. There was no one terrible cause of Fiona's unhappiness, or an awful dark secret in her life.

They got a taxi back to Fiona's place. The taxi driver was listening to the radio and Will suddenly realized that it was a discussion about Kurt Cobain.

'What's happened to him?' Will asked.

'He shot himself in the head. He's dead.'

Will wasn't surprised, and he was too old to be shocked. It wasn't unusual for pop stars to kill themselves. But then he thought about Marcus and Ellie, and that worried him. What would they think?

'Isn't he the singer Marcus liked?' Fiona asked him.

'Yes.' Suddenly Will was afraid. He didn't know why, but he had a strange feeling that Marcus might be in trouble.

'Can I come in with you?' he asked Fiona when they arrived at her house. 'Perhaps Marcus has left a message on your answer machine. I just want to hear that he's OK.'

There *was* a message from Marcus, but he didn't sound OK. He was calling from a police station in a town called Royston and he sounded frightened and lonely.

◆

Ellie had started drinking vodka on the train, and Marcus was feeling very tired. Whenever people stared at her, she started shouting at them and saying that she would stop the train.

Marcus was beginning to realize that he didn't actually want Ellie to be his girlfriend. She was funny and pretty and clever, but she just wasn't the right kind of person for him. He needed to be with someone quieter, someone who liked reading and computer games. Ellie's behaviour was frightening and embarrassing.

'Why does Kurt Cobain's death matter so much?' he asked her quietly.

'I loved him.'

'You didn't know him.'

'Of course I knew him. I listen to him every day. I wear him on my sweatshirt every day. He understood me. He knew what I felt, and he sang about it.'

Marcus tried to remember the words of some of the songs on the Nirvana CD that Will had given him for Christmas, but they didn't mean anything to him.

'So how were you feeling?'

'Angry.'

'What about?'

'Nothing. Just ... life. Life's awful.'

Marcus thought about that. He realized that Ellie spent her whole time wanting life to be awful, and making things difficult for herself. School was awful for her because she wore her sweatshirt every day, which wasn't allowed, and because she shouted at teachers and got into fights. But why didn't she stop doing those things? Her life wouldn't be so awful then.

'Do you feel like shooting yourself?' Marcus asked.

'Of course. Sometimes, anyway.'

Marcus looked at her. 'That's not true, Ellie.'

'How do you know?'

'Because I know how my mum feels. And you don't feel like that. You have a nice life.'

'I have an awful life.'

'No. *I* have an awful life. And my mum has an awful life. But you ... I don't think so. I'll tell you, you don't feel anything like my mum, or Kurt Cobain. You shouldn't say that you feel like killing yourself when you don't. It's not right.'

They sat in silence. Marcus was looking out of the window of the train, wondering what he was going to say to his dad about Ellie. He didn't notice that the train had pulled into Royston station. Suddenly Ellie stood up and jumped off the train. Marcus waited for a moment, then, with a horrible sick feeling, he jumped off after her.

'What are you doing?'

'I don't want to go to your dad's. I don't know him.'

She walked out of the station and Marcus followed her. They walked up a side road and on to the High Street, past a chemist and a supermarket. Then they came to a music shop with a big **cardboard** figure of Kurt Cobain in the window.

'Look at that,' said Ellie. 'That's really terrible. They're trying to make money out of his death.'

She took off one of her boots and threw it at the glass window of the shop as hard as she could. The glass broke first time. Ellie reached inside and took out the cardboard figure of Kurt Cobain. She sat down outside the shop, holding the figure and smiling a weird little smile.

'Oh, Ellie. What did you do that for?'

Once again, Marcus had the feeling that Ellie didn't have to do what she'd just done. She didn't have to make trouble for herself. He was tired of her behaviour. There was enough trouble in the world without inventing more.

The street had been quiet when Ellie broke the window, but the noise of breaking glass had woken Royston up. Some people ran down to see what was happening.

'Right, you two. Stay there,' said a guy with long hair who looked like a hairdresser.

'We're not going anywhere, are we, Marcus?' said Ellie sweetly.

cardboard /'kɑːdbɔːd/ (n) very thick, strong paper, often used for making boxes

6.1 Were you right?

Look back at your answers to Activity 5.4. Then tick (✓) the true sentences below.

1 ☐ **a** Will has stopped telling lies.

☐ **b** Will has become more selfish.

☐ **c** Will wants his life to change.

2 ☐ **a** Marcus and Ellie go to Cambridge.

☐ **b** Ellie gets upset on the train to Cambridge.

☐ **c** Marcus breaks a shop window.

6.2 What more did you learn?

What are these people saying? Write the correct letters.

1 ....

2 ....

3 ....

4 ....

5 ....

6 ....

A 'I thought we were friends.'

B 'I want to help you.'

C 'Life's awful.'

D 'I'm sorry for being like this.'

E 'Yes, but I'm not your dad.'

F 'You have a nice life.'

6.3 Language in use

Look at the sentences in the box.
Then rewrite the sentences below
with *when*.

> **When Marcus went to find Ellie in her classroom at breaktime,** she didn't seem very pleased to see him.
>
> 'Can I come in with you?' he asked Fiona **when they arrived at her house**.

1 Marcus told Will about Fiona, but Will wasn't very helpful.
   When *Marcus told Will about Fiona, he wasn't very helpful* .

2 Will and Fiona met in a pub and then Fiona told Will about her problems.
   Fiona ....
   ....

3 Marcus saw the newspaper and then started worrying about Ellie.
   When ....
   ....

4 Ellie jumped off the train and Marcus followed her.
   Marcus ....
   ....

5 Marcus was embarrassed because Ellie broke the shop window.
   When ....
   ....

6 Some people heard the noise, so they ran down the street.
   Some people ....
   ....

6.4 What happens next?

Will all the main characters be happy at the end of the story? What do you think? List them under these headings.

- **Happy:**

   ....

- **Quite happy:**

   ....

- **Unhappy:**

   ....

CHAPTER 11

Growing Up

He was looking at real life and seeing what it was like to be human.
It wasn't too bad, really.

A police car took Marcus and Ellie to the police station. The policemen were nice really. Ellie had explained that she wasn't a troublemaker or on drugs; she was angry because the owner of the music shop was making money out of Kurt Cobain's death. The policemen thought this was funny and laughed, which made Ellie even more angry.

When they got to the police station, they were taken into a little room and a policewoman came in and started talking to them. She asked them their ages and addresses, and what they were doing in Royston. Marcus tried to explain about his dad and the big think and Kurt Cobain and the vodka. But the policewoman couldn't understand the connection between his dad's accident and Ellie and the shop window.

'He didn't do anything,' Ellie suddenly said. 'I got off the train and he followed. I broke the window. Let him go.'

'Let him go where?' asked the policewoman. 'We've got to phone one of his parents. We've got to phone yours too.'

The police telephoned Marcus's dad and Ellie's mum. Then Marcus rang Fiona, but she wasn't in, so he left a message on her answer machine.

They sat and waited in silence until Marcus's dad and Lindsey arrived. Neither of them was in a very good mood. Lindsey had had to drive, because of Clive's broken arm, and she hated driving. His dad was in pain. He didn't look like a man who had had a big think or wanted to see his only son.

The policewoman left them alone and Clive sat down on a seat that ran along one side of the room. Lindsey sat down next to him. Marcus looked at his dad unhappily.

'He didn't do anything,' said Ellie impatiently. 'He was trying to help me.'

'And who exactly are you?'

'*Who exactly?* I'm Eleanor Toyah McCrae, aged fifteen years, seven months. I live at 23 ...'

'What are you doing with Marcus?'

'He's my friend.' This was news to Marcus. He hadn't felt that Ellie was his friend since they got on the train. 'He asked me to come with him to Cambridge because he wasn't looking forward to talking to you.'

Marcus put his head in his hands. He was suddenly very, very tired. He didn't want to be with any of these people.

'I suppose you think all this is my fault,' said Clive. 'If I had stayed with your mother, you wouldn't be in trouble.'

'What are you talking about?' said Marcus. 'What's happened? I just got off a train.' He wasn't tired now, but he was beginning to feel angry. 'What's wrong with getting off a train? Ellie's crazy. She broke a window with her boot because it had a picture of a pop star in it. But I haven't done anything. And I don't care if you left home or not. It doesn't make any difference to me. I just wanted to try and look after my friend.'

Ellie laughed. 'Cool speech, Marcus! Can we go now?'

'We have to wait for your mother,' Clive told her. 'She's coming with Fiona. Will's driving them up from London.'

'Oh, no,' said Marcus.

The four of them sat there staring at each other, like characters in a play without an ending.

◆

After the police had called Ellie's mum, she had called Fiona. Then Fiona spoke to Clive, then she called Ellie's mum and offered her a lift up to Royston with her and Will. Ellie's mum was an attractive woman in her early forties. She didn't seem surprised or upset about her daughter's problems.

When Will, Fiona and Ellie's mum arrived at the police station in Royston, Clive and Lindsey were staring angrily at Marcus, Marcus was staring angrily at the wall, and Ellie was staring angrily at everyone.

'Can we go now?' Will asked the policewoman.

'Not yet. We're waiting for the shop owner to come. It's something we're trying here. Criminals meet the **victims** of their crimes, so they understand the effects of their actions.'

'Good,' said Ellie. 'I want to see what this person's like.'

A nervous-looking young woman in her twenties was shown into the room. She was wearing a Kurt Cobain sweatshirt and lots of black eye make-up and she looked like Ellie's older sister.

'This is Ruth, who owns the shop. This is the young lady who broke your window,' said the policewoman.

Ellie looked at Ruth, very surprised. 'Did they tell you to look like me?' she said.

'Do I look like you?' Ruth asked.

Everyone in the room laughed, including the police officers.

'You put that picture in the window to make money,' said Ellie, but she didn't sound as confident as before.

'Which picture? The picture of Kurt? That's always been there. I think he's great. Is that why you broke the window? Because you thought I was trying to make money out of Kurt's death?'

'Yes.'

'Today has been the saddest day of my life. And then a stupid little girl breaks my window because she thinks I'm trying to get money out of people. Just ... grow up.'

Ellie was very embarrassed and didn't know what to say. 'I'm sorry,' she whispered.

'All right,' said Ruth. 'Come here.' She opened her arms, and Ellie stood up, walked over to her and hugged her.

Suddenly, Fiona, who had been very quiet, got up too, walked around the table, and put her arms round Marcus.

'I haven't been a good mother to him,' she said to the policewoman who had been looking after them. 'I haven't been noticing things. I know I don't deserve another chance, but I'm asking for one ... If you give us another chance, you won't be sorry.'

'We don't need another chance, Mum,' said Marcus. 'I haven't done anything wrong. I only got off a train.'

victim /ˈvɪktɪm/ (n) someone who has been hurt by something

But Fiona took no notice of Marcus. She was mad, thought Will, and she was saying crazy things, and nothing could stop her. But he knew she had suddenly realized that she had to do something for her son. And if she was thinking that, then she wasn't going to try and kill herself again.

'Please let Marcus go,' Fiona said, and put her face in Marcus's neck.

But Marcus shook her off and moved away from her and towards Will. 'You're mad, Mum. I can't believe how mad both my parents are,' he said with real feeling.

Will looked at this strange little group and tried to make some sense of it. He couldn't understand these people. He hadn't known some of them before today; he had known some of them for only a short time, and he couldn't say that he knew them well. But here they were anyway, one of them holding a cardboard figure of Kurt Cobain, one of them crying, one with a broken arm, all connected to each other in different ways. Will couldn't remember being involved in this kind of situation before. He was looking at real life and seeing what it was like to be human. It wasn't too bad, really.

◆

Marcus went to stay with his dad and Lindsey in Cambridge that night. In the car Clive complained a lot about Ellie and what had happened. Why did Marcus want to be involved with someone like that? Why hadn't he tried to stop her? Marcus didn't say anything, and finally his father was quiet. Later, when Lindsey had gone to bed, he and Marcus talked.

'I've had a big think, you know, since my accident,' said Clive. 'I know I haven't been a very good father. And ... you need a father, don't you? I can see that now.'

'Why do you think I need a father now? I'm doing OK without one.'

'It doesn't look like it.'

'What, because Ellie broke a window? No, really, I am doing OK. Maybe I'm doing better. It's hard with Mum, but this year at school ... I can't explain it, but I feel safer than before, because I know more people. I was really frightened because I didn't think two people were enough, but now there aren't only two. There are lots.'

'You mean Ellie and Will and people like that?'

'Yes.'

'It was wrong of me to leave you,' said his dad. 'That's what my big think was about.'

'It doesn't matter, Dad. I know where you are if things get bad. I'm OK. Really. I can find people. I'll be all right.'

And he would be all right, he knew it. He didn't know whether Ellie would be, because she didn't think about things very hard. And he didn't know if his mum would be, because she wasn't very strong a lot of the time. But he was sure he could cope in ways that they couldn't. He could cope at school because he knew what to do, and he had learnt who you could trust and who you couldn't.

They talked a bit longer, about Lindsey, and how she wanted a baby, and how his dad couldn't decide, and whether Marcus would mind if they had one; and Marcus said he liked babies. And then his dad gave him a hug and he went to bed. In the morning his dad and Lindsey took him to the station and gave him enough money for a taxi from King's Cross back to the flat.

◆

Will knew that his feelings for Rachel had changed his life for ever. He wanted her so much that it frightened him. He was terribly afraid of losing her; perhaps she would get bored with him, or meet someone else. He wasn't Will the cool guy who didn't want to get involved with other people now. He was deeply involved with Rachel, and he couldn't go back. He wanted to be an important part of her life, and to make her think of him as a responsible person. So he started taking Ali and Marcus out on Saturdays, sometimes to football games but usually to the cinema and McDonald's.

In some ways Marcus seemed older than Ali now. He dressed better – he had won the argument with his mother about whether he could go shopping with Will – and he had his hair cut regularly. He was still good friends with Ellie and

Zoe, but he was more careful about what he said to them, and they didn't laugh at him as much.

It was strange; Will missed him. Marcus was the only person in the world who might be able to give him advice, but Marcus – the old Marcus – was disappearing.

'Are you going to marry my mum?' Ali asked one day, when they were eating chips at McDonald's.

'I used to want him to marry *my* mum,' said Marcus. 'I thought it would solve all our problems. Your mum's different, though. She's not as confused as my mum.'

'Do you still want him to marry your mum?'

Will stared at them both in disbelief.

'No,' said Marcus. 'I don't think it would help. You're safer as a kid if everyone's friends. Think about it. Your mum and my mum are friends.' It was true. Rachel and Fiona saw each other regularly now. 'And Will sees my mum, and I see you, and Ellie and Zoe, and Lindsey and my dad. There are lots of people now.'

One afternoon, when Will took Marcus back to his flat, Marcus disappeared into his bedroom with a quick 'thanks'.

'He seems so much older,' Fiona said.

'Yes,' said Will. 'Are you worried about that?'

'Why do you ask? Of course I am.'

'But ... you've seemed better recently.'

'I think I am. I don't know why, but I think I'm more in control of everything.'

Will thought he knew one of the reasons, but he didn't want to hurt Fiona's feelings. The truth was that the new Marcus wasn't so difficult to look after. He had friends and he could look after himself. He was just like every other twelve-year-old boy.

Marcus came out of his room. 'I'm bored. Can I get a video?'

Will decided to give Marcus a little test. 'Hey, Fiona. Why don't you get your music out and we can all sing a Joni Mitchell song?'

'Would you like to?' asked Fiona.

'Yes, of course.' But Will was watching Marcus's face carefully. Marcus was looking really embarrassed.

'Please, Mum. Don't.'

'But Marcus, you love singing. You love Joni Mitchell.'

'I don't. Not now. I hate Joni Mitchell.'

Will knew then, without any doubt, that Marcus would be OK.

1 Look back at your answers to Activity 6.4. **Think about Marcus and Will at the beginning of the book and at the end. Complete the table (✓ or ✗). Then compare your ideas with two or three other people. Do you agree with each other?**

	At the beginning		At the end	
	Will	Marcus	Will	Marcus
selfish				
kind				
lazy				
worried				
strange				
cool				
'grown up'				
happy				

2 **Work with two or three other students. Choose one of these characters: Fiona, Will or Marcus. Imagine that character in five years' time. Discuss the questions and make notes. Then talk to other students. Do you all agree?**

Notes

1 What does he/she do now? (e.g. a job)
2 Has he/she got a boyfriend/girlfriend/husband/wife?
3 Does he/she live in the same place?
4 Has he/she got the same friends?
5 Has he/she made new friends?
6 Is he/she happier than before? Why (not)?

1 Prepare a short review of the book. Make notes under these headings.

About a Boy

by Nick Hornby

The main characters
Describe Marcus, Fiona and Will.
What do they look like?
What kind of people are they?

....
....
....
....
....
....
....
....

The main story
Why did Will first meet Marcus?
How did they become friends?
How did they eventually help each other?

....
....
....
....
....
....
....

Lessons from the story
Do you think that any lessons can be learnt?
If so, what are they?

....
....
....
....
....
....
....
....

Your opinion
Is it a sad book? Is it funny?
Is it a good story?
Should your friends read it? Why?

....
....
....
....
....
....
....
....

Book Review: ☆☆☆☆☆

2 Now write your review on another piece of paper.

Project *Problems, problems*

1 ***About a Boy*** **is a story about different people and their problems. Work in small groups and discuss these people's problems. What advice or help were they given? What did they do about the problems?**

2 **Match the advice below with the people in exercise 1.**

You are ill. Don't wait to get better by yourself – you need help now. You need to talk to somebody, and you might need some pills. You should see a doctor, who will be able to give you the best advice.

Moluptat wis nullan vent lum nulla feu fac' ... ommy   luptat, con v inim ilit

You seem very confident and cheerful, but really you are worried about yourself. Have you thought about making changes to your life? You could go out and do something interesting – why don't you get a job? Then you will feel better about yourself … and people will like you more!

Is there anybody who you can talk to? Maybe a teacher, or a relative? You shouldn't have to worry about all this by yourself. And remember, you are not the only person who feels alone sometimes. Relax! You will soon make some friends.

3 **Discuss whether you agree with the advice.**

4 **What kinds of problems do young people have? Talk about older teenagers – between 15 and 19 years old. Make a list of problems. Then decide if the problems are easy to solve or not.**

Teenage problems
- No friends
- Bullying

5 Work with another student. Read the two letters below. Make notes about the problems each person has.

LETTERS OF THE MONTH

Problem page letters

I'm eighteen and I've just started college in a new town, hundreds of miles away from my family home. I don't know anybody and I'm finding it difficult to meet people and make friends. I'm missing my family a lot. I'm quite shy and feel nervous about talking to new people. I'm interested in lots of things, but they're mostly activities I do alone – painting, reading, walking, playing computer games, playing the guitar. How can I make new friends and stop feeling homesick?

jackhobson@jh811.hotletter.com

I am a sixteen-year-old girl who loves clothes and fashion. The trouble is, I can't afford to buy all the stuff I want. A few months ago I started stealing from shops. At first I just took little things, but it got easier and easier. Now I've got a cupboard full of stolen shoes, dresses, skirts and trousers. I never wear them, but I'm really worried that somebody is going to find out and I'll go to prison.

Chantelle Jacobs, London

Notes   Jack   Chantal

6 Choose one of the people above, either Jack or Chantelle. What advice would you give him or her? Discuss your ideas and complete these sentences.

You should

Why don't you

What about

You could

Have you thought about

Don't

91

7 Look at your notes from exercises 5 and 6. Now write your advice in a letter.

Dear

I've read your letter, and this is my advice.

I wish you lots of luck in the future!
With best wishes